Notes On a Wet Cocktail Napkin

Memories of Bernard's Surf... and Beyond

By

Rusty Fischer

Founder and CEO of

Rusty's Seafood & Oyster Bar

WingSpan Press

Published in the United States and the United Kingdom

by WingSpan Press, Livermore, CA

The WingSpan name, logo and colophon are the trademarks of WingSpan Publishing.

ISBN 978-1-63683-034-6 (pbk.)
ISBN 978-163683-498-6 (hardcover)
ISBN 978-1-63683-972-1 (ebk.)

First edition 2023

Printed in the United States of America

www.wingspanpress.com

Table of Contents

Dedication

There is a notation at the bottom of every business check I sign that reads, "This Check Made Possible By Tourism". It is a gentle reminder, to our vendors, to our staff, and often to myself, of why we're here and how blessed we've been to come so far since it all began in a sleepy seaside fishing village so very many years ago.

In that same vein, this book is sincerely dedicated to the customers, the work family and friends whose support over the years made Bernard's Surf, and this book, possible. From the bottom of my heart, I thank you sincerely and hope you enjoy this fond look back at the memories you helped create!

Acknowledgements

They say it takes a village to raise a child. Well, it certainly took a packed dining room's worth of folks to help me gather, collect, collate, fact check, remember and sort through all the memories you are about to digest!

Honestly, though, this book would not have been possible without the immeasurable help of a select group of individuals who were there from the beginning of this long-simmering project. From folks who were there during the Surf's heyday to folks whose parents were there, from employees past and present, from friends to family and everyone in between, here then are some people I would like to formally recognize for their help in getting this book into your hands:

Juli Shroble, for providing a boat load of pictures that took me straight down Memory Lane and back again! Thanks for all your support over the years, and I hope you enjoy the finished product!

Jane Vester, for long, lingering lunches during this project's infancy that helped nudge the project along and steer its course in the right direction.

Charlie Ragland, for reminding me of stories I'd long forgotten, and filling in the blanks for those I thought I'd remembered so clearly. Your loss affected us all, and this book literally wouldn't have been possible without your help.

Larry Garrison, for writing a whole chapter of this book – and saving me the trouble of coming up with a few dozen more memories to fill its pages. Honestly, though, you will be missed more than you could ever imagine.

Bruce Arrow, for also writing most of a chapter of this book on the "County Boys" and Wickham Road and for always being there for me, to this day.

To John Quinn, former editor for *USA Today* and respected journalist, who helped fine tune my chapter on Al Neuharth and provide valuable insight about the man so influential in both of our lives.

To Colee, for the gift of our two boys.

To Sherrell, for the gift of Jack.

To Phyllis, for the gift of kindness and compassion.

To Ana Rivera, for printing about a dozen copies of this book over the years so I can make sure every word is just right!

To Dana Mrdjenovich, for energetically and competently steering the Rusty's organization to newer and greater heights every year, always with an eye on the future while never forgetting the past.

To Jack King, widely considered 'the voice of NASA' during the Apollo years, for his invaluable contributions to the space program during its earliest, and most vulnerable, years.

To Bev Kasimier and Ken Fisher, both of whom continued to encourage me to finish this book even during a long and challenging year full of loss and change. It might not have been easy to push through at the time, but I appreciate your efforts now that the day is finally here.

To Tom Alston, who was our insurance representative for Bernard's Surf, for getting me appointed to the Cape Canaveral Hospital Board, which has lasted some 40 years. He also convinced my father, Lou, to finally sell me Bernard's Surf, so let's thank him twice!!

To my brother, Ronnie, who passed away just before we completed the final edits of this book. He was more than just a business partner over the years, or even a brother, but a friend and companion in good times and bad. He, along with my sister Dorsay, both passed within a year of each other, leaving behind family, friends and memories to last a lifetime.

To the whole Rusty's team, for always having my back and making sure there are always enough coasters at the ready and plenty of crackers on the bar! I'm hoping that this brief glimpse into the Surf history and all its glory can help you understand why the little details are so important.

And, last but not least, how can I forget John Alexander, for keeping on me about finally getting this book into print and out in the world. First copy of it goes to you, my friend, that's for sure!!

Prologue

Liftoff!

May 5, 1961.

You know you've grown up on the Space Coast – or even during the Space Age – if that date means something special to you. (And if not, don't worry; it will in a moment.) As a junior at Melbourne High School that year, the date didn't mean much more to me than the standardized test we were taking in the crowded auditorium that morning.

There we sat, row after row, lined up in peg jeans and madras shirts, with buzz cuts to keep our heads cool in the sweltering Florida heat. A proctor lectured us from between the endless rows of desks, stating quite clearly that if we were to leave the room for any reason – *any* reason at all – we would fail the test.

No ifs, ands or buts.

Well, it wasn't his fault; he had a good reason to be strict that day, of all days. Set to launch that morning from nearby Cape Canaveral was the Freedom 7 Mercury capsule, carrying none other than Alan Shepard himself. If all went well, and we all prayed that it would, Shepard would be only the second man – and, most importantly, the first American – ever to travel into space.

"Let's Go!"

We all knew about the launch, of course. The buzz had been building for weeks in our little seaside community, and up and down the Space Coast itself, to say nothing of the rest of the country. Living a stone's throw from the launch pad, it was easy to take for granted that we would soon see history firsthand as a rocket would shortly be soaring into the blue Florida sky right over our heads.

As each minute of test-taking drudgery brought us closer to liftoff, you could feel the energy in the old Melbourne High auditorium surge. It was like a growing buzz of electricity, a liftoff of our very own, counting down in our young, restless bodies as we all began fidgeting and looking around the room for the signal.

What signal? Little did the proctor know it that day, but all around the room "lookouts" had been stationed at strategic locations. Or maybe they should have been called "listen outs," since their weapon of choice wasn't binoculars or magnifying glasses, but tiny transistor radios, tucked discreetly into a pocket here or a purse there, tuned not to the hottest rock 'n roll station of the day as usual, but the launch details coming out of nearby Cape Canaveral.

Feet were squeaking anxiously on the auditorium floor, knees bobbing up and down nervously, pencils tapping restlessly on half-finished answer sheets as the countdown went through its usual delays.

And then, finally, the signal came. At around 9:33 that morning, as the countdown finally began in earnest, with T minus one minute and counting, sentries up and down the rows of carefully lined desks began signaling the rest of us about the approaching launch.

Someone, I can't remember who anymore but I can picture them clinging to a transistor radio, earplug firmly wedged in his or her ear, smiling triumphantly, stood up, chair legs squeaking on the varnished floor, and announced the two words we'd been waiting for all morning: "Let's go."

Liftoff !!!

One by one, we joined him. Chair legs shot out in unison as we stood up like soldiers being called to attention and fled through the side auditorium doors, which opened onto a large grassy plain. You could already feel the rumbling of the giant rocket lifting into the air, even if you couldn't quite hear it yet.

Then, it came; long, loud and, in years to come, unmistakable – a rocket launching from mere miles away. The boom rumbled through the air, thrilling all, shocking some, moving others to tears as we stood, joined by our shared awe at the miracle of science we were witnessing in the clear blue Florida sky just above our heads.

Back then, it was such a new sound. Like a controlled explosion, roaring and rumbling through the sky, I'm sure many of us thought something had gone wrong. And God knows it could have. At the time I thought Shepard was just about the bravest guy on the planet for being the first American launched into space, but thinking back on all that could have gone wrong that day, I've reassessed that to read the bravest guy in the *universe*.

Only one man had gone into space before him, a Soviet cosmonaut named Yuri Gagarin, only a month earlier. So there Shepard sat, on a massive metal cylinder filled with rocket fuel, not knowing what to expect beyond the many simulations he must have endured before his big day on the launch pad.

Anything could have happened, at least in our amazed teenage minds as we looked ever upward to witness the impossible happen right above our heads.

Would the missile blow up? Veer wildly once off the launch pad? Or go as high as it was supposed to go? As fast as it was supposed to? And that was just the launch. But what about the landing? Would Shepard come back where he was supposed to, in the Atlantic Ocean? In one piece? Or would his capsule sink to the bottom?

Would he come back at all?

None of us knew the answers to those questions that fateful morning, least of all Alan Shepard. Necks craned, on the tips of our toes, we simply stared above the football bleachers at the clear, blue sky. Murmuring amongst ourselves, hands shielding the sun, eyes straining for a better view and then, it happened – the first shriek announced what we'd all been waiting for: the clear yellow burn of a rocket screaming through the sky toward space, that final frontier.

It burned above the powerful roar, leaving a tight, white trail behind it that signaled its path and told us what we were seeing was real. This was really happening. Alan Shepard was going into space, and our families, our friends, our parents and neighbors had helped put him there.

As I recall that day the bright yellow fire burned until it disappeared behind a cloud, leaving only the tight white trail behind, coiling into itself as the rumble and roar continued for a few seconds more. Then, the flame was gone, the white contrails fading until they might have just been clouds, the Florida sky silent and blue once more.

Back to the Future

We lingered for a few moments, a few of us fighting tears, and all eager to bask in the shared triumph of America's historic moment for as long as possible. We had just witnessed history, and weren't very eager to give up our front row seats.

But you could only stare at an empty blue Florida sky for so long before reality crept back in. So, one by one, we dutifully returned to the auditorium. There the Proctor waited, red-faced but silent, as we sank into our chairs and, heads low lest we be called out first, returned to our tests.

I remember the white paper and black dots seemed so dull then, after watching the bright blue sky and roaring yellow fire that morning. And as we sat there, waiting for the hammer to fall, for the Proctor to call us out of the room, one by one, nothing happened.

What could he do? Fail us all? In the end, the test, and the rest of the school day, passed uneventfully. The same could not be said for the rest of the 1960s and 70s, even the 80s, 90s and beyond, to this very day. While the American space program had already existed for years, May 5, 1961, was the day the whole world noticed, and nothing would ever be the same again.

While those of us lucky enough to live on the Space Coast watched it live and in person, millions watched it on their televisions at home, all across the country. It was the beginning of the Space Age, a period of unparalleled growth, exploration and success for America, in general, and NASA, Cape Canaveral and the Space Coast in particular.

President John Kennedy's dreams of space exploration succeeded beyond his wildest dreams, not only above the earth but right here, on the Space Coast itself. In pursuit of Kennedy's ambitious goal of "landing a man on the moon and returning him safely to the earth" by the end of the 1960s, the area virtually exploded with contractors, scientists, engineers, technicians and, come launch days, national TV personalities such as Walter Cronkite and David Brinkley.

For better or worse, the world would watch our shores – and our skies – religiously for the next few decades, and I would find myself

4

inextricably linked not just to the space program, but to the Space Coast itself.

Growing Up in the Shadow of Rockets

So much of my later life, so much of all *our* lives, is linked to that fateful May morning back in the early 60s. One day my own children would go to Freedom 7 Elementary School, named after the space capsule that carried Shepard into orbit during that historic mission and that later splashed down into the Atlantic Ocean, signaling his safe return back to earth – mission accomplished.

Every December my family and I gather for a little pre-holiday sushi at a restaurant located at the hotel once owned by several of the original Apollo astronauts, including "Gus" Grissom, John Glenn, Walter Schirra and, of course, Alan Shepard. (It's a La Quinta now, but many old-timers like me will recall it by its original name, the Cape Colony.)

And, just a few short years after that first American manned launch into space, as the new owner of a restaurant called Bernard's Surf, I'd have the opportunity to personally shake Alan Shepard's hand and welcome him as a guest to the restaurant.

To *my* restaurant.

But more on that later…

This isn't a book about Alan Shepard, per se, or even about the many space missions that followed. But it *is* about his spirit of adventure, the spirit of the Space Coast itself, and the spirit of the brave men and women who not only soared into space but designed the rockets, paved the landing strips or built the launch pads that sent them there.

They became our neighbors, our friends, our sons-in-law and fathers-in-law and even daughters- and mothers-in-law! In later years, they became good and loyal customers and people I'm proud to call my friends.

Bernard's Surf opened its doors in 1948, when Cocoa Beach had a population of only a few hundred people and was little more than a few paved lots running up and down a sandy stretch of road known as A1A. It was, in short, a boom town just before the boom:

Liftoff to Prosperity

And what a boom it was! Thanks mostly to the space program and the federal money being poured into Cape Canaveral to the north and, to the south, at Patrick Air Force Base, Cocoa Beach's population increased dramatically from 1948, when Bernard's Surf first opened its doors, through the 60s – and beyond. And "the Surf," as locals called it, was there, front and center, for the whole ride.

Engineers and electricians, laborers and rocket scientists, support and clerical staff, custodians and executives, soldiers and sergeants alike moved to Brevard County because of the space program and often stayed because of the Space Coast and all its various amenities. And what amenities they were: long, unbroken stretches of white, sandy beaches, swaying palm trees, clear blue skies, plenty of sunshine and a tropical climate that barely skipped a beat during the winter months.

This book is about that ride, that boom, and those people. I was only five years old when my uncles Bernard and Sidney opened the Surf, so it's been a part of me virtually all of my life. So has the Space Coast, its people, its employees, its ups and downs, tragedies and triumphs, heroes and scoundrels. I've served them all, or so it would seem, at one time or another.

So whether you were born here, grew up here, winter here or are just traveling here for the first time, I hope you'll enjoy this front row view of a community quite unlike any other.

I should know. You get to learn a lot about a town and its people, even its guests, while running a restaurant. And now you'll know what I know when you read my very own *Notes on a Wet Cocktail Napkin...*

Chapter 1:

The Beginning of a Tradition

No book on Bernard's Surf, or even the Space Coast itself, would be complete without at least a *little* history. And though my father Lou and his brothers Bernard, Sidney and Eddie – the original "Fischer Men" – are long gone by now, the memories – and their legacy – still remain.

In fact, years ago I asked my dad to recount those early years of Cocoa Beach and Bernard's Surf for a monthly newsletter the Surf used to publish called, appropriately enough, *The Surf Sounds*. Dad willingly obliged, and turns out Dad knew how to turn a phrase as well as run his own fishing fleet.

So here, in his own words, is how Dad recalled those earliest years of Cocoa Beach and the grand opening of a brand new restaurant in town known as… Bernard's Surf:

On October 31, 1948, a sleepy village of several hundred residents called Cocoa Beach awoke to the excitement of something new going on next door to the old Post Office.

Bernard's Surf was about to open its doors, and a dream of Bernard Fischer was about to be realized. So on that Halloween night, the doors opened to a packed house, wall to wall people enjoying the delicacies prepared by "Mama Fischer," mainly her chopped liver pate and other goodies. All the Fischer brothers tended bar that night, in support of Bernard's new venture.

It was a memorable occasion. In addition to local residents, many friends drove over from Cocoa, Merritt Island and Melbourne.

Bernard's Surf started as a bar lounge and package store, [where] the only food served was hors d' oeuvres and sandwiches. The whole operation was housed in what was then the current bar and lounge…

I can clearly picture my father standing proudly behind the bar that night, pouring draft beers or measuring out two fingers of Scotch – okay, maybe three fingers – with his own hands, smiling with a trademark pipe hanging out of his mouth and his sleek white hair slicked back.

A fisherman by trade, Dad was a brother first and a businessman second. It was just like he and his brothers Sidney and Eddie to help Bernard out on his big night, though I can't imagine my father working a full shift before the lure of steamed shrimp and the comfort of a cozy leather booth called him away for a shift drink – or two – of his own!

A Personal Recollection of Opening Night

Of course, I was only a kid at the time the Surf opened its doors in 1948, with little inclination as to how the restaurant would impact my life for the next 70-plus years – and still is to this day.

But we are fortunate to have another recounting of that historic occasion written by a live eyewitness in the form of Bob Grothe, the Surf's original manager.

Bob was there that night, rolling up his sleeves and working closely alongside Bernard and his three brothers to feed and water an overflow crowd that filled the restaurant, spilled out into the street and, by all accounts, partied through the night in downtown Cocoa Beach, where the Surf was conveniently located.

Here, in his own words, is how Bob tells the story of that fateful evening so long ago:

In 1948, the road to Cocoa Beach from Cocoa was a two-lane highway having two draw bridges, which were often out of order. However, on opening night, they were working perfectly. Engraved invitations had been sent to all of the professionals, political figures and VIPs in the area.

Promptly at 7 p.m., the doors were opened to a waiting crowd. The back bar was filled with beautiful bouquets of flowers wishing the Fischers the best of luck.

The women wore formal gowns and the men, semi-formal. The bartenders were uniformed in white jackets and black bow ties. The hostess was Nellie Roe Lynch and Lois Botner was the head waitress.

Among the hors d' oeuvres served was an initial 200 pounds of jumbo shrimp, steamed in beer, which was consumed so rapidly that an additional 300 pounds had to be sent for.

The turnout was so great that emergency tables were set up outside on the sidewalks to serve both the food and cocktails, with the party lasting until midnight. It was a night to remember, and that's the way I remember October 31, 1948, opening night of the first Cocktail Lounge on Cocoa Beach.

Though I wasn't physically present, pictures remain to document the historic occasion and as I stare at them now, it's amazing to think that while so much time has passed, in some ways so little has changed.

There's Bernard behind the bar in one such picture, long since faded from black and white to a stiff, yellowish-brown. In the photo he's young and handsome and full of promise, handing a customer a drink with a proud, beaming smile on his face as he stands behind the bar.

Correction: stands behind *his* bar.

There's the overflow crowd Bob was talking about in another picture (you can find all the pictures I'm talking about in the middle of this very book), pressed up against cars in the parking lot, leaning against telephone poles and the original black and white "Surf" street sign, eating steamed shrimp off paper plates in the street, cups of beer at their feet. Far from the regal and elegant crowd Bob describes inside, these revelers were perhaps a more authentic representation of the changing times: blue jeans and t-shirts and young, hopeful smiles.

The scene reminds me of so many of the holiday block parties we used to have over the years in downtown Cocoa Beach, the children and nephews of those original guests no doubt lining the very same streets, eating paper plates full of steamed shrimp of their own decades later. It makes me proud to be part of that legacy, and grateful to Bernard for being the original architect of so many cherished family memories.

In yet another black and white picture fading into yellowish-brown, the old Surf lounge is crowded with smiling faces, cigarettes and drinks all around, heavy leather booths crowded to well over capacity as opening night stretches into opening morning.

And that's how I'd always known the Surf growing up: heavy leather booths reeking of cigarette smoke, the big, long bar the minute you walked in, a cast of characters spending their days or nights – or both – telling wild stories or hoisting me onto a barstool for a soda or a "kiddie cocktail," made of 7-Up, grenadine and heavy on the maraschino cherries.

Before the Surf, There Was a Town...

Cocoa Beach wasn't even a city when Bernard opened it in 1948. Established in June of 1925, it wasn't officially incorporated until years after the Surf opened, in 1957. It was just a sleepy seaside village back in those days, but it grew quickly. According to CityOfCocoaBeach. com, "During the moon-boom years, from 1960s to 1970s, the City saw an increase in population by 286.39% (3,475 to 9,952)."

One of the town's earliest residents was Jesse Casbon and his family. According to his son and my good friend, John, Mr. Casbon came to Cocoa Beach in 1946 with $7,500 cash in his pockets, a small fortune by 1940s standards.

Like many northern transplants, Mr. Casbon saw Cocoa Beach as a boomtown waiting to happen, a gem on the Space Coast that wasn't quite the Space Coast yet, nor quite a polished diamond, either. He knew it had potential to be much more than a "sleepy fishing village," as it was so often called, and Mr. Casbon went right to work either buying up – or building up – the heart of downtown Cocoa Beach around the sandy, scruffy intersection of Minuteman and A1A.

Mr. Casbon got right to work by building the first of several properties in the mid-40s and beyond. With lots costing between $750 and $900 at the time, he was in the right place at the right time to be an ambitious young family man looking for his part of the American dream.

He started reshaping downtown Cocoa Beach with the building that was eventually to house Bernard's Surf, crafting it from the ground up, on the property at 2 South Atlantic Avenue. John and his brother and sister actually lived in the completed building as children, in a town with so few kids there wasn't even a school yet. In fact, when John Casbon was born he was the 42nd citizen of Cocoa Beach... ever.

Mr. Casbon was a barber by trade, and came to Cocoa Beach to set up shop and make a new start. Unfortunately, the wheels of progress moved so slowly in the tiny city government back then that it took him forever to get a barber's license to cut hair legally.

In the meantime, he cut hair for free and waited to get a license, watching the town grow all around him and wanting to be a part of the pioneer spirit that the tiny seaside town offered its handful of full-time residents.

After he built the structure that was to eventually become Bernard's Surf, Mr. Casbon moved his family inside and they all lived there while he built another home for them just across the alley between the two buildings.

John can still remember living in the room that was eventually to become the office of the "old" Surf, where local legends Ana Mae Petit and Norma Shroble would work and teach me most of what I knew about the Surf in years to come. It was in the back corner, facing south down A1A.

Back then, the Surf held far less square footage than it did when I took over in the 1960s. In fact, at the time, there was no "red room". Instead, the plot of land that was to become the red room was just a scruffy lot of old Florida brush pines, which was what John looked out on each night.

His only neighbor at the time was an old woman named Mrs. Kimberly, who lived in a small apartment complex where the Surf office would eventually stand – and where Subway is today.

Mrs. Kimberly had a strange and fascinating hobby, one that John now recalls fondly: at night she would go to the hotel across the street and sit there and watch the flashes in the sky over the Atlantic Ocean. They weren't fireworks or even the sunset, but the gun flares as US naval ships fired on German U-Boats off the coast during World War II!

In her front yard was a unique flower pot, an old, unexploded shell that had washed up off the beach and which sat at the entrance to her apartment, flowers sticking out of the top.

In those days, Mr. Casbon didn't have a customer in mind for the Surf yet, nor was it designed to be a restaurant... just a bar, which the growing – and thirsty – little seaside town sorely needed. That is, at least according to Mr. Casbon, and obviously my uncle Bernard agreed.

As John tells it, his dad was looking to sell the building at 2 South Atlantic Avenue to someone in the fishing business because, back then, they were the only ones with enough cash on hand to actually buy it for the price his father was asking.

That's why, when the building was finally finished, Mr. Casbon set about pursuing Bernard… or at least one of the "Fischer men," well known in the local community as avid fishermen and, more importantly, successful businessmen. He wanted someone from the fishing industry to own the place, and when it came to seafood in those days, few names were as synonymous with fishing as the Fischer name.

Little did Mr. Casbon know that Bernard had more in mind for the little building on the corner of Minuteman Causeway and A1A than raw shrimp and bait fish, although both were to play a big part in its success.

A Future Landmark on Shaky Ground

For me, I suppose, the Surf had always been a part of my life, even if only on the sidelines. For the entire Fischer family, it was like an extended living room. Birthdays, celebrations, anniversaries, retirements, holidays, graduations, were always celebrated at the Surf – and I'm proud to say that we weren't alone.

For generations families have turned to the Surf as their "go to" spot for such celebrations. But if the Fischer brothers had bailed on Bernard's big gamble back in 1948, the Surf might have never gotten off the ground in the first place. And they came very close to bailing indeed.

As a young kid growing up, to me the Surf had always seemed busy, popular, successful, the place to go and always crowded, but I later learned that it wasn't always that way. In fact, for its first few years, the Surf was on very shaky ground indeed. Here's how Dad recalls the story of the Surf's earliest and, perhaps, darkest and most uncertain years:

Unfortunately, Bernard's dream proved to be a few years premature. There was little growth on the beach during those first few years the Surf was in business, and too small a population to support the business [without it].

As a result, the Surf lost money during the stagnant growth period, but Bernard's faith in the future of Cocoa Beach was unshaken. (And, as we were about to soon learn, with good reason.)

He appealed to his brothers, Sid, Lou and Eddie to continue to finance the operation. They were all engaged in the seafood business known as Fischer's Seafood.

The brothers continued to support Bernard in his struggle for survival. After the first few years, things finally started to turn around. The space program was announced, so Bernard's faith was soon to prove him right.

Over the next few years the Surf would eventually expand into a full restaurant, quickly becoming the focal point in the development of Cocoa Beach...

Having witnessed a few of my own bright business ideas crash and burn over the years – more on those later – I can only feel Bernard's pain as he struggled through those dark times in the Surf's first few years in business, walking that fine line between giving up and sticking to his guns, with nothing but faith and his family to keep him afloat until his ship came in.

Even once the Surf was mine and well into the 1980s and 90s, there were still lean years to come and, thankfully, go. I often experienced the same lean times and self-doubt as my uncle Bernard did. It's not easy dodging phone calls from the bank every day or wondering how you're going to cover payroll next week, so I know all too well how Bernard felt during those first few years as the Surf struggled to find its legs, and its customers, as our "sleepy fishing village" came into its own as a bona fide resort town. And it couldn't have been easy borrowing money from his brothers, either.

Still, we're all glad he did. And soon, all of Cocoa Beach would be as well:

Meals So Special, Even the Menus Are Souvenirs: *Launching a Fine Dining Restaurant on the Space Coast*

After the announcement of the space program that was designed to ultimately carry a man to the moon, it was several years before Cocoa Beach finally started to show signs of the coming boom that Bernard had been waiting for since opening the Surf several years earlier. But by

1950, the Space Coast was finally beginning to "catch up" to Bernard's prediction that it would soon be a boom town well-served by Cocoa Beach's "first cocktail lounge".

That was the same year that the first rocket launched from Cape Canaveral. According to NASA.gov, "A new chapter in space flight began on July 1950 with the launch of the first rocket from Cape Canaveral, Fla.: the Bumper 2..."

In anticipation of the coming space boom, Bernard started building his own "space program" of sorts, expanding both the size of the restaurant's dining area as well as the kitchen.

Perusing through some old menus I found in storage recently, several dating all the way back to the late 50s and early 60s, I'm amused by not only the prices listed, but the variety – and ambitiousness – of menu items the newly expanded kitchen was forced to prepare as Bernard and his Surf expanded from its humble beginnings as "the Surf Cocktail Lounge" to what would ultimately become "Bernard's Surf Cocktail Lounge and Dining Room."

Everything from "hot" crab claws ($1.50, and that included French fried potatoes, coleslaw, hot breads, butter, coffee or tea!) to filet mignon ($3.95), broiled South African lobster tails ($4.50) and jumbo frog legs ($2.45) plus Maryland fried chicken ($2.95 and from a recipe dated back to 1890!)

Borrowing from the international flare that colored the wide array of foods both foreign and domestic, the dessert menu featured the traditional, like ice cream and lime sherbet for a quarter, to the cosmopolitan like Camembert, Liederkranz and Gruyere cheeses for .35 cents each. And a hot, frothy cappuccino or demitasse after your meal would only run you a cool .25 cents!

In addition to the wide variety of foods offered with an international flare, the menu cover promised a variety of other amenities, such as an "air-conditioned lounge" and "excellent mixed drinks." True to tradition, the menu also boasted – and truthfully – that "all seafoods served here are caught by our own fleet of boats." (Take that, Red Lobster!)

As my father Lou Fischer would later recall in an article entitled "Launching a Restaurant" from another issue of the *Surf Sounds*:

As business started picking up, there was not enough seating to handle the crowds, so Bernard built what is now called the Red Room. Even this added seating capacity could not handle the business, but Bernard ran out of real estate, and had to do the best he could with what he had...

What Bernard had was quality, service and a fierce desire to satisfy every customer who walked through the door. Bernard wasn't content to operate anything less than a fine dining establishment, and his commitment to quality was never in doubt. Old photos show Bernard working the restaurant floor in a dapper suit and tie, holding one of his famed menus in hand. His staff was equally as formal, at least back in those days, with his chef wearing the appropriate white jacket and chef's hat and servers in full uniform.

Over time Bernard developed – and developed and re-developed – the constantly evolving menu that became a national conversation piece, endorsed by *Gourmet* magazine and Vincent Price, who once told Bernard, "It's terrific!" Excerpts of the new Surf menu even appeared in Walter Winchell's newspaper column.

No wonder. For Bernard, dinner was like a Broadway show – something to be savored, enjoyed, not rushed and always very, very special – and the menu was like a Playbill; he wrote, designed and printed them accordingly.

Trust me, these menus are like taking a trip back into time. No one makes menus like this anymore, for the simple reason that you couldn't afford them these days.

Oversized, always colored a rich red or a sleek black, printed on heavy card stock and laminated to a durable glossy finish for multiple uses night after night, they were definitely suitable for framing. The almost sumptuous cover featured the famous "Surf" logo spelled out in cursive, along with a picture of a loaded down shrimp boat labeled "Fischer's Seafood" and bearing the Fischer Men's logo, "From Our Fishing Fleet to You."

To open it is to spend the next twenty to thirty minutes perusing the "specials" alone, to say nothing of the regular meals printed directly on the menu itself. (Which could account for why folks tended to take so much longer to eat back then!) All around the borders inside the menu, postcard size labels were stapled – by hand – to show off the weekly specials.

Surf hostess Norma Shroble's daughter, Juli, remembers one of her first ever "Surf" jobs was writing out – by hand – the different card specials to be stapled all around the menu. At the time, I'm guessing the early 60s if I'm not mistaken, she got 75 cents a menu, which considering the number of squares stapled to every available inch of border space of the huge menu, was a steal at the time.

In true Bernard style, each nightly special begins with the phrase, "Bernard Fischer Proudly Presents," and his detailed and almost luxurious menu reveals just how proud he was to feature such dishes as Baked Danish Lobster En Casserole ($5.50), Giant Shrimp Stuffed With Maine Lobster Dressing ($4.50), Green Turtle Steak ($3.75) or his famous "Mariner's Delight," featuring a "shrimp boat full of shrimp, oysters, scallops and crabmeat sautéed in butter" ($4.50). Thanks to Ms. Shroble, the prices were handwritten to reflect the freshness of the ingredients and the fluctuating nature of the market prices for fresh seafood from that era.

Thanks to its exotic contents, rich printing and wide variety, customers regularly wanted to buy the menus (which cost the Surf $2 each to print) and mail them to their friends all over the country as souvenirs. The demand was so great that Bernard decided to charge a minimum of $3 per menu, which he promptly donated to the Cape Canaveral Hospital Building Fund.

When they learned where their dollars were going, most customers reacted by paying $5 to $10 to take home a menu, and I'm told some larger donations were also made over the years. As a result, Bernard raised thousands of dollars for the hospital fund and left behind a powerful legacy of charitable giving that I'm proud to honor to this day.

Changes on the Horizon

With the Surf expanding and nearly bursting at the seams as the growing space program continued to turn Cocoa Beach into the boom town Bernard had always predicted, changes were in the future for the Surf as well.

Uncle Sidney left the seafood business for good in order to join Bernard in the operation of the Surf full-time. He became a valuable asset, relieving Bernard of detailed functions of the day-to-day business

– and just in time. This left Bernard free to do the things he loved the most, such as developing new dishes and personally looking after his customers' needs as he circulated around the crowded dining room each night, dressed to the nines in a three-piece suit and greeting each guest in turn.

Unburdened from most of the demands in the "back of the house," Bernard continued to finesse award winning dishes from his busy kitchen and add them to his first-rate menu. There were broiled scallops almandine ($3.95), sautéed Chilean Langostinos with sherry ($3.95), shark steak ($3.50) and a customer favorite, Doc Stahl's Special, featuring shrimp, crabmeat, mushrooms and wild rice sautéed in garlic butter ($3.75).

Along the way Bernard eventually became a world class host, entertaining well-known personalities from the space and military fields, broadcasting and national and foreign governments. A few celebrities that I can remember Dad telling me visited the Surf over the years include Arthur Godfrey, Huntley and Brinkley, Walter Cronkite, John Chancellor, Werner Von Braun, Kurt Debus, Edward G. Robinson, David Janssen, Gregory Peck and many, many more. (More on those famous guests, and many others, later in the book.)

What I loved about Bernard, and only saw second hand, was that he never lost sight of his regular guests. Those folks who are there for you day in and day out, year after year, sitting at your bar on a slow Tuesday afternoon in August or September, helping you make payroll every week with their draft beers and fish sandwiches and early bird specials.

Despite his eagerness to build a world class brand with "international" flair, Bernard was even more interested in serving world class meals to appreciative customers, whoever they were.

This meant he was also truly celebrity blind, and anyone who walked through the door was a "guest," whether it was Gregory Peck or just plain "Greg," the local mailman, cop or janitor. According to Bernard they all deserved the same service and, more importantly, the same respect.

Bernard's aim was to please, his dream was to give folks the night of their life, no matter who they were or why they were there. Birthday party, graduation or just another Monday night, it was all the same – and all special – to Bernard.

As Dad recalled it, "Bernard, although impressed by the famous ones, never gave them preference over his regular customers, first time visitors, tourists or anyone else who came in. To him, one customer was just as important as another, regardless of his status in life."

I like to think I ran the Surf the same way during my day and must have, because many was the time an excited waitress, bartender or manager had to point out a famous face as I toiled behind the bar or worked the floor... with no earthly idea who they were, or why they were famous in the first place!

A Bar... Or a Bank?

In those early days of dirt roads and residents numbering in the hundreds, not thousands, there were no banks or chambers of commerce in Cocoa Beach, and there were certainly no ATM machines or debit cards. As a result, the Surf became the de facto local bank, city hall and information bureau.

There was always a long line of workers waiting to get their payroll checks cashed in the package store every Friday afternoon, and Sidney was certainly a godsend to the many newcomers moving to Cocoa Beach: when moving vans would arrive and were not permitted to accept checks, after asking around people would ultimately call on Sidney or Bernard for help in getting their possessions loaded into their new homes. To my knowledge, these newest residents of Cocoa Beach were never turned down.

The Fischer brothers helped many, many people with their financial problems over the years and, as a result, sent the message that Cocoa Beach was a fine place to live, work and play.

As a commercial and information center, the Surf was the meeting place for local developers, real estate operators, lawyers, accountants and anyone else who needed to know what was what back in the day.

Years before City Hall was built (and even after construction was finished), the Surf lounge was the unofficial "city hall," where its very first power brokers, including my Uncle Sidney (who would later serve as the first elected mayor of Cocoa Beach from 1956 to 1960 and later have a city park named after him), would sit over drinks and conversation, literally building a town out of beach sand… and from scratch, scribbling out rough blueprints, sketches and ideas on the only writing material they had handy: wet cocktail napkins.

But it wasn't just the locals who benefited from the little cocktail lounge's thriving pulse. The Surf, in the form of brothers Bernard and Sidney, furnished information and guidance to anyone who asked. Even today, I have people tell me about the favors extended to them by Bernard, Sidney – or both – at some point over those early years of both the restaurant, and a growing community.

Bernard continued his charity efforts by holding two Chinese auctions each year for the March of Dimes. Volunteers would solicit items from merchants and conduct the auction. Some of the auctioneers I can remember read like a "Who's Who" of Cocoa Beach movers and shakers: future Commissioner Paul Godke, future Mayor Bob Murkshe, future Commissioner Tom O'Conner and future Commissioner Tom Gavin.

The Surf always donated part of its receipts for the event, as well as dinners and bottles of liquor to be auctioned off. The auctions became very popular events for a worthwhile cause, and continued to cement the Surf not just as a business, but as a *family* business – and the community was truly part of that family.

It wasn't just local charities who benefited from Bernard's generous spirit, but the "locals" themselves. Every year on Halloween night, the Surf's anniversary, Bernard would give away steamed Canaveral shrimp as a "reward" for his loyal customers. It was a way of saying "thank you" to the residents of Cocoa Beach and the Space Coast, a tip of the hat and show of appreciation for their patronage over the previous year and, hopefully, many more years to come.

The event grew exponentially, revealing not just how the little surf town was growing but how much it had come to depend on the Surf as its central hub of community activity. That first year, 500 pounds were consumed, and each year after the demand increased by a few hundred pounds or more.

When the order finally reached 1,800 pounds, Bernard called a halt to the annual Halloween tradition. Turns out even one of the most generous men in Cocoa Beach had his limits, and 1,800 pounds of fresh, savory, market-priced shrimp was my uncle's!

Surprisingly, this halting of the annual standing room only, boiled shrimp free-for-all was mainly at the request of many of his regular customers, who couldn't even get inside the restaurant to eat on their favorite night of the year!

It seems that most of the people who actually came out to eat the giveaway appetizers were not, in fact, Bernard's regular customers but merely hungry opportunists who stopped by once a year to line their stomachs, purses, pockets or whatever else they could cram with free shrimp for the taking.

For his part, Uncle Sidney entered politics as a way to help the community and keep the Fischer Men front and center in local business dealings. He served as a member of the City Commission, and later became the first elected mayor of Cocoa Beach.

He served several years in that position before stepping down to play politics "behind the scenes," a job he excelled at for many more years to come. In his honor, a city park, Sidney Fischer Park, was named after him. Sidney was too ill to attend the opening ceremonies, so his wife Irene accepted the honor on his behalf.

Colonel A. M. "Chick" Davis, who was an engineer with the US Air force, told me that Sidney, as mayor in the mid-50s, was a great help to him in clearing the way to make A1A a four-lane road through the heart of Cocoa Beach, and also in bringing the good water that we enjoy today.

You could still drive on the beach back in those days, and thank goodness for that. Before the space program took hold and even in the Surf's first few shaky years, Cocoa Beach needed more than just endless miles of uncluttered coastline to draw tourists and Floridians alike to its growing number of shops and restaurants.

Racing on the beach proved the key to those early days of both Cocoa Beach's and the Surf's success. Every year the Surf sponsored two big racing events and both weekends the streets of Cocoa Beach were full of the year's latest models of race cars.

Long before the Daytona Speedway was built, Cocoa Beach offered both miles of unspoiled coastline – known as "the world's greatest speedway" as early as 1924 – and, once the race was over, a new watering hole right across the street from the beach to cool off the parched lips and hungry stomachs of drivers and fans alike. As always,

Bernard was there behind the bar to welcome the thirsty crowds inside the packed bar, a sight that never failed to make him smile.

It was just the jump start the Surf needed, and those events – as well as the community goodwill and free marketing that they offered – helped Bernard keep the Surf afloat in those early, vulnerable years before rockets taking off from nearby Cape Canaveral helped jumpstart Cocoa Beach's "space boom" years. The annual events helped build the Surf brand beyond the Space Coast and helped make fans of new and old customers alike.

Life went on like that, the Surf establishing a foothold on not just the corner of Minuteman Causeway and A1A, but in the community of Cocoa Beach itself. As the 50s turned into the 60s, life on the Space Coast had changed quite a bit from those uncertain days when Bernard first opened the restaurant and waited for the "boom town" to catch up with his own entrepreneurial spirit and unceasing vision.

Now rockets were becoming a bigger and bigger deal, and the Space Program had seen that "small community of a few hundred residents" explode into a full-fledged city full of engineers, techs and support personnel and their families.

No longer did Sidney and Bernard have to loan out money to new residents or old. Banks had sprung up all over town, as had motels and bars and lounges and even a host of competing restaurants. Regular launches brought in big numbers of tourists and newsmen alike, and many visitors to the Space Coast found it so appealing they simply never left, sticking around and putting down permanent roots instead.

Through it all, the Surf continued to grow, expand and stick to its original tenets of excellent service, quality food and a seat at the table for all comers. But times were changing, for the Space Coast, for the country, for the Fischer brothers and, especially, for me.

The undisputed reign of hosts Bernard and Sidney would soon come to a close, and my time to assume the Surf legacy was almost at hand. But you sure could have fooled me. At the time, I was just another teenager with a buzz cut and thick glasses, tossing the ball around with my brother Ronnie and hanging around with pals from school.

But the family business finally called, in unexpected and unfamiliar ways.

Chapter 2:

Another Fischer Man

Contrary to popular belief, I wasn't born in a suit and tie, walking around the Red Room checking on tables or asking Cosmonauts to sign the Surf menu in between shots of chilled Stolichnaya. In fact, my first "job" at the Surf happened quite by accident.

Naturally, I'd brought my prom date to the family restaurant before going to the big dance that night. The Surf was busy with the usual weekend crowd, but when I walked in Bernard stopped everything to come over and say "hi" to me and my date.

Unfortunately, I soon found out why.

"Rusty," he said, voice sounding uncharacteristically stressed. "We've run out of pumpernickel rolls for the bread baskets. Can you run by Eli's Bakery and pick up a few dozen so I don't have a mutiny on my hands by dessert? I promise I'll have your table ready by the time you get back…"

What could I do? My family needed me more than my date at that moment, so back into the car I hopped, shiny blue rented tux squeaking against the leather seat of my old jalopy.

I zipped down a block or two to the Bailiwick Mall and pressed Eli into action, picking up Bernard's hastily placed order and saving the day when I made a triumphant return back to the restaurant, several bags of still warm pumpernickel rolls in each hand.

The dinner rush – and prom night – saved, Bernard rewarded my date and I with the best seat in the house. I would like to say that Bernard "paid" me for the effort with a free meal, but instead I'm pretty sure I charged it to my dad's house account… and left a tip out of my own pocket! (So I guess that was more of an unpaid internship than a real job.)

Okay, so that wasn't a real "job," but it always felt good to help the family out in times of need, even if it was just to pick up a few rolls before prom! But my first real job working for the family had nothing to do with the restaurant at all. In fact, it was a lot more about catching fish on a hook than it was serving them on a plate.

The Fischer Men (which consisted of my father, Lou, and his brothers, Bernard, Sidney and Eddie) have a long and storied history in the world of catching, and serving, seafood. While my uncles Bernard and Sidney ran the Surf, my dad took care of the seafood side of the equation.

With a small "fleet" of local fishing and shrimp boats moored at nearby Port Canaveral, Dad and his trusty captains provided the fresh seafood for which Bernard's Surf had become famous. "From our fishing fleet to you" was no simple boast or made-up tag line just for the giant Surf menus.

An article written on the four original Fischer brothers for the *Orlando Sentinel* back in the 50s details the financial reach of the actual fleet the original "Fischer Men" were responsible for back in those early days.

Boasting "The Fischer fleet is the largest on Florida's east coast," the *Sentinel* article goes on to explain, "The family now owns four deep sea trawlers, has a financial interest in another 25 shrimp boats and unloads 200 boats a year at the four fish houses…"

Of course, the Port looked very different in the fifties and sixties than it does today. The fact is, what we know as the "Port" today didn't even exist back when the Fischer brothers started operating there in the early 1940s. Instead, there was a single Oceanside wharf, north of the Jetties, where local seafood companies, including Fischer's Seafood, offloaded their daily catch.

Back then the shrimp and fishing boats would pull up to the wharf, offload their catch and then set anchor just offshore. The Fischer operation was a pretty big deal in those days, with a processing plant right at the base of the old Canaveral wharf and even an assortment of fishing cottages.

What is now deep water and home to a massive cruise and cargo industry, to say nothing of the SpaceX fleet, was once miles and miles of dusty scrub brush, like so much of "old" Florida. But as the wheels of progress turned and the years marched on, eventually the

Port was dredged and the seafood business boomed, bringing access and thousands of pounds of fresh fish, shrimp, scallops and more to a convenient and modern location. Just like Bernard reaped the benefits of a booming Cocoa Beach before them, the Fischer brothers were poised to make the most of the Port's expansion as they, too, grew their already busy operations to new and unforeseen heights.

There were no restaurants at the Port to speak of back then, no Cove district or Disney cruise ships or observation towers or walking trails or sightseeing helicopters or glimpses of mock Crew Dragon capsules on the backs of SpaceX ships. Just a row of single-story fisheries where hardworking men and women toiled from early morning until sunset in shrimp boots and rubber aprons processing the fresh shrimp, scallops, oysters and endless varieties of fish the boats brought in all day long.

Dad owned one such processing house, located in the vacant building just north of Fishlips. In those days the docks weren't lined with tourists or waitresses bearing trays of margaritas, or even cozy decks to sit on.

Instead they were clogged with boats fresh from – or on their way back out to – the sea, and fishermen climbing on or off the slippery decks and smelling like the deep sea itself. The smell of gurgling diesel oil and the shouts of sunburned men grateful to be heading home filled the air, dawn to dusk, week in and week out, year after year.

I would go there often over the years, watching hundreds of pounds of fresh shrimp swinging from metal scales while fish by the ton swam by on giant conveyer belts to be processed before sold at weight to (then) popular local restaurants like the Surf, George's Steakhouse, Ramon's or The Mouse Trap. But soon I would be on the other end of the scale: crewing for one of the few charter boats then operating out of the port:

"From Our Fishing Fleet to You"

It was my first summer job, ever, and my first ever job working for my family. I was crewing for the charter fishing boat my father Lou owned and it was my first taste of what Bernard and Sidney meant by their famous slogan on the front of every menu, "From our fishing fleet to you."

Aboard his trusty ship The Miss Charleston, Captain Earl Brinson kept things running smoothly from the wheelhouse while fellow deck mate Johnny Johnson and I did the usual grunt chores aboard a charter fishing boat: baiting lines, untangling them, cleaning up the vomit from seasick guests, untangling more lines, baiting more lines, then washing down the deck some more.

In those days the sea was ripe with all kinds of fresh fish, from giant grouper, snapper and flounder to pompano, Mahi and tuna. The Miss Charleston chugged out to a few miles offshore, dropped anchor and then we helped the guests, up to two or three dozen would-be fishermen and -women, drop their lines and reel 'em in.

Day after day, the sun beat down as the fish piled up. We'd tag them for each fisherman or fisherwoman and ice them down, then run back and bait some more hooks before tagging some more fish and baiting more hooks, until we could do it in our sleep – and occasionally did (or so it seemed). The ship would gently rock, then *not* so gently rock. You got used to it, or you got sick and cleaned up after yourself, *then* got used to it. Either way, you didn't really have a choice.

First mate Johnny Johnson and I prayed for gentle days, merely because fewer waves meant fewer trips back and forth to wash some seasick guest's stomach contents from the deck with a fresh bucket and mop.

The seas would rock and churn as the boat drifted in search of fresh fishing holes sure to make for satisfied customers. In rare moments between icing down fish or baiting hooks, we could stare down into the blue-green water or snag a cold bottle of Coke from the cooler and watch the unspoiled coastline stretch for miles and miles of condo-free beaches as far as the eye could see.

It was hot and tiring but I got to interact with folks who, later that night, would more than likely be dining at the Surf. (They might even be eating their own fish!)

You could say it was my first "customer service" role in the family business, except that the customers didn't pay me much mind and were far more interested in how quickly I could put raw squid on their hook and get it back in the water for them than they were in hearing about the nightly specials my uncle Bernard might be featuring that night.

I would like to say it was a charming and rustic experience that

I hold dear to my heart to this day, but I honestly remember it a tad differently than that. Mostly it was hot and smelly and tiring and I couldn't wait to get back to the dock every day.

The Miss Charleston left the Port promptly at eight every morning and returned at five in the evening, meaning we showed up to get everything ready around seven and stayed, hosing down fish blood and scales off the decks and stowing the lines and rigging until around six in the evening.

Probably my favorite part of the day was hoisting the massive fish onto hooks at the dock and watching proud fishermen pose with their catch. They still do that at the Port today, and watching it always brings me back to the days of disposable flash bulbs and thick sunglasses and the giant fish we hung, crushed ice dripping from their slimy scales, day after day, all summer long.

Although they launch from a different location now, it's strange and also familiar to look out my office window above Rusty's at the Port and watch the crews of the local charter boats run fairly the same routine as I did nearly 50 years ago back when I was a sunburned teenager myself.

The only difference is now, when the crews cluster around the tiki bar at Rusty's at the Port after a long, hot day on the boats, I can occasionally stop by and buy them a drink, remembering how thirsty I'd get that long, hot summer of 1963 (when I was still too young to drink, let alone buy, a beer).

Dad eventually sold off the Miss Charleston, as well as the rest of his fishing fleet, and Captain Irl and Johnny and myself moved onto bigger and better things.

Johnny Johnston was big into conservation and went on to pursue his passions for saving both the coastline and the environment. In fact, if you ever visit the nature preserve at Lori Wilson Park, you can admire some of Johnny's handiwork.

After all, the nature trail is named after him! In another connection, Johnny's wife Sophie worked in our retail seafood market for pretty much as long as I can remember.

The Boys of Summer

After a summer on the high seas, I was ready for a change of pace.

Little did I know that, trading in my deck shoes and bait hooks for a shovel and hard hat, I'd wind up in an even hotter, harder, longer job – and for several years running!

It's easy for us to drive to work or out to dinner and forget that the roads we're on are often named after folks who served our communities above and beyond the call of duty, especially when we're stuck in traffic! Anyone who's ever tried to get from Point A to Point B on Wickham Road in Melbourne during rush hour has probably prayed for an alternate route, but if it wasn't for one man, Joe Wickham, we'd probably still be stuck in traffic on a dirt road.

Joseph F. Wickham moved to Brevard County in 1926, when he was still in his teens. He graduated from Eau Gallie High School in 1929 and got his start on the (mostly unpaved) streets of Brevard delivering soft drinks fresh out of high school. Later he learned land surveying from his father and mastered the construction field while serving in the Navy, supervising the building of runways and air strips in the South Pacific. Back home, he started a construction company of his own in the 1940s and later served as a County Commissioner for 26 years.

Well, that's the "official bio," anyway (courtesy of RootsWeb.com). Personally speaking, I knew Joe mostly from the summer jobs he'd save out for local teens like myself, helping to pave Wickham Road and do other odd jobs for the county.

In the summers of 1964 and 1965, I was lucky enough to get on a road crew with my school buddies Bruce Arrow, Richard Dunn, Kim Hammond and his brother Bill, Bruce Jacobus and others as we worked alongside older, more veteran county workers turning Melbourne's dirt roads into major thoroughfares and side streets for the good folks of Brevard.

It was a great job for us young guys, seeing as the regular road crews – or, as we called them, the "County Guys" – did most of the heavy lifting and "us kids" were mostly there for support. Most of my days, as I recall, were spent in the cab of a truck backing it up or pulling it forward as often as a bucket operator needed me to.

I can keenly remember digging the basin for what would eventually become the lake at Wickham Park and racing dump trucks with my pals to empty out the sand we dug from the giant hole that grew bigger and bigger each day.

While we never actually clipped any trees in the process, not big ones anyway, we came close more times than I cared to remember. And at the end of the day, Wickham Park had a lake to be proud of and nobody was any the wiser! (Until now, I suppose.)

The job paid good money, which both of the Bruces, Kim, Bill and I promptly spent as soon as we earned it, drinking our troubles away each night. After a long day of work paving the city's roads we'd head straight to the beach, washing the grime and sweat and dust of the day off in the waves at the end of 5th Avenue in Indialantic.

Afterward we'd successfully badger someone old enough into buying us a six-pack or two before heading home for a quick shower and then back out for the night, tooling around town looking for action or some trouble to get into – or usually both. Then it was right back to work the next morning to do it all over again.

Of course, it's not the work I remember so much after all these years, but the cast of characters the boys and I worked alongside during those hot and hazy summers in that crazy time known as the 60s.

Then again, my memory's not exactly what it used to be. Thankfully, my old friend Bruce Arrow's *is*. Now a happily married man and retired insurance executive, I'm thankful to my old pal Bruce for providing a brief sampling of the local color we enjoyed during those long, hot summers. Here is how Bruce recalls the "Boys of Summer," circa 1963 and 1964:

Bruce Jacobus was the boss's favorite. Bruce, I believe, worked a full summer before any of us and was considered more mature and responsible. Over time, he became a fomenter of discontent and led the famous July 4th work stoppage and return to the barn. [He also] organized many Friday, after work trips to Gainesville to see [our friend] Alden and arrange for the rest of us to cavort with assorted loose women.

Bill Hammond was a short timer. He didn't like to work hard or sweat much. [He] quit as a County Boy after a short stint.

Kim Hammond maintained his "good boy" image at all times. Stayed pretty much aloof from the rest of the County Boys and did not open his dinner box in the company of the "Regulars," thereby missing much of the colorful commentary. As a result he was allowed to operate the Wabco/Westinghouse pan. As I recall, he did not avail himself of the full four-year opportunity.

Richard Dunn was best known for his one opportunity to escape ditch cleaning and root throwing. He was given an opportunity to drive the wheeled dragline to the barn. He failed to secure the bucket and when he turned the corner to the barn, the bucket swung out and took the top off a Volkswagen Beetle!

Hutch Stewart drove the other Farmall tractor, usually paired with Ronald Fender. One day he encountered a redneck man beating his woman with a loaf of bread. When he tried to intercede on behalf of the woman, they both turned and attacked him!

Bruce "Moe" Arrow was probably the most colorful of all County Boys! His escapades are legendary. While throwing roots from a dirt right of way on a near 100-degree day, he was approached by [County regular] "the Preacher," who asked him if he could drive a truck. At the time, Bruce couldn't even drive a stick shift car.

He answered, "Yes!" So Preacher shouted, "Jump in, I'm taking you to the barn!" On the way, Preacher revealed that the truck had 15 gears, including under drive and over drive. Moe was scared but undaunted. Preacher put him in a WWII surplus dump and took off. Moe fooled with the gear shift briefly and started up. The clutch popped and the truck lurched and bucked.

Moe reached for what he thought was the hand brake, which turned out to be the dump lever. Instantly, the truck dump body engaged and went straight up.

Milt ran out of the barn and instructed me on the gears and sent me off to the marl pit to haul marl. On the way, I stuck the truck twice and then backed around a pile of marl and went tail down into the pit. Herman Cason cussed Moe for five minutes and then pulled him out with a front loader.

The most notorious act of dereliction occurred on a paving job on South Patrick Drive. Moe was assigned to flag traffic on a one lane stretch of about 200 yards. He was just coming off a wicked bender and was totally hung over.

When he stepped forward to check the far flagman... he dropped the flag and a little old lady in a new yellow Cadillac hit the gas and knocked him unconscious into a drainage ditch. He was later offered enough insurance money to put him through college twice, but his mother turned it down!

One thing I do remember clearly is something that came to be known as the "Great 4th of July Standoff." At least, in my mind anyway. Back then we kids were always looking for a quick and early escape from the day's heat. And anyone who's ever worked outside in the heat of a long, Florida summer can agree with us.

We used to live for the sign of one of the County Men, nicknamed "Pop," who was always first back to the barn at the end of the day. Whoever was closest would yell, "Quittin' time! Pop's heading back to the barn." It was our unofficial whistle blow and the signal that the long, hot day was finally over.

In the early 60s, of course, Wickham Road looked very different than it does today. Back then, as I recall, there was little past Pineda Causeway to the north other than cow fields and humid pastures of endless green grass.

None of us liked to work weekends or holidays, particularly since we all felt work was just an interruption to more pleasurable jobs like goofing off at the beach, drinking beer or chasing loose women!

One 4th of July the "boys of summer" all agreed that there was no way we were working the entire day. Fireworks were to be seen, beer was to be drunk, girls were to be chased. We wouldn't stand for the injustice, no way, no how.

So we agreed that, come lunchtime, instead of returning to our jobs after eating bologna sandwiches out of our metal lunch pails like every other weekday, we'd just head back to the barn instead and knockoff for the holiday.

Of course, none of us thought to ask our boss, Bill Prince, if we could knock off early. (Probably because we knew the answer would be "no.") So in our college boy minds, we figured if we led a revolt, nobody would be able to do anymore work. It was the 60s, after all, and while we might not have been long-haired "hippies," we were certainly not against a well-intentioned protest now and again. Especially if it was for something we really believed in, such as working half-a-day. We probably thought the County Guys who worked the roads year in, year out, would thank us.

But as lunchtime came and the revolt, led by my old pal Bruce Jacobus, started in earnest, a serious-minded foreman ran out to meet us on our way back to the barn. "You boys get back to work," he commanded, or words to those effect, "or you'll all be fired."

Well, with a few weeks of summer left and plenty of high-grade pay on the line, we all wimped out. Back to work we went, ending the short-lived "rebellion" before it ever really got off the ground. But all was not lost, after all. A few hours later, with the spirit of our mutiny still hanging in the air, the foremen called us all in and told us we could go home.

4th of July had been saved!

Let the fireworks – and drinking – begin!

Excuse Me, Officer...

Life was just different back then. Simple, easy, uncomplicated. People were friendlier, more neighborly. I'll never forget the time I was training for the Junior Olympics back in high school. The competition was stiff and required a lot of training, and I committed myself to it like I did everything athletic back then: nonstop and full bore!

I was about 15 at the time and living with my father in a little house across from the Tides apartment complex on South 11th Street in Cocoa Beach. Part of the competition was to see who could run a mile the fastest, and of course I was in it to win it!

So every day after school I would walk across A1A and straight past the dunes onto the beach and run the fastest mile I possibly could. Or, at least, what I thought was a mile. After guessing a few times I worried I might not be running the full distance. But how to find out? Well, I finally got smart. This was way back in the day. Not only was the beach flat and wide enough to run across it without pulling a hamstring in the soft sand of the uneven dunes, but you could still drive on it back then.

As I was about to start running my training mile one day, a police officer came driving by. I waved him over and said, "Excuse me, Officer, but I'm training for the Junior Olympics and could use some help."

"How can I help?" he asked, without hesitation.

"Can you drive up a ways and, when you get to a mile, draw a line in the sand for me so I'll know how far to go?"Just like that, the officer agreed and drove straight off. Sure enough, as I ran and ran and ran, there was a freshly drawn line waiting there in the sand for me at the end of a mile. At the time, I thought nothing of it. That's just how Cocoa Beach was back in the 50s and 60s. I suppose the rest of the world was that way as well.

Now you'd probably get cited for a "nuisance call" if you asked for such a thing, but at the time... it was just another day in sunny Florida. As a small footnote, I'm proud to say that I *did* go on to win every competition for the men in that year's Junior Olympics, and I owe at least some recognition to that random police officer for helping me know just how far a mile was in the sand of a long ago distant Cocoa Beach.

Chapter 3:

College, Interrupted

My days on the Wickham Road crew are fondly recalled, as are my days as an FSU Seminole. I'd been offered an athletic scholarship to attend Florida State University and play football as a college freshman, but a wicked knee injury during my senior season had sidelined me the entire summer after graduating from Melbourne High School.

Rather than cutting bait on the Miss Charleston or raising cane with my pals Bruce Arrow, Bruce Jacobus and the Hammond brothers paving Wickham Road for another summer, I worked out in the gym, rehabbed my knee and by my freshman year at FSU I was cleared to play, my athletic scholarship saved at the last minute!

Of course, I didn't see much action as a third-string quarterback for the 'Noles. (And no, for the record, I never played with Burt Reynolds, who was sidelined by knee injuries in his 1957 season – nearly 10 years before I got there.) Still, I enjoyed being on the team and attending classes at FSU with most of my old pals from Melbourne High.

But after two years of warming the bench, I decided to leave the Noles, move out of Smith Hall and into an off-campus apartment with roommates – and old friends – Bruce Arrow and Richard Dunn. There were still adventures to be had in between business classes, and plenty of them occurred at the SAE house with my other fraternity brothers. (Enough to fill a whole other book, I imagine, but for that... you'll have to wait for the sequel!)

Duty officially called in the summer of 1965, however, and my pals and I returned home to toil for another summer for Joe Wickham and his County Boys turning cow pastures and sand lots into paved roads.

Or so I thought.

But in May of that year, after only a week or two of sweating and digging on the County job, my father, Lou Fischer, came to me and asked if we could talk. Dad was usually the silent type so, this being a not-so-common event, I knew something big must have happened.

I just could never have guessed *how* big at the time.

Turns out, Dad wanted me to start working at the Surf. Full-time, immediately, and by the way… would that be okay with me? Apparently, Bernard hadn't been feeling well lately and Lou wanted someone in the family to be there keeping an eye on the place and a finger on the pulse of things until Bernard felt better. Pulse? You want to talk about pulse? Mine was racing at the sudden news, to say nothing of the enormity of Dad's request.

Naturally, I felt intimidated at first. The Surf was a big place, and an even bigger responsibility. And I was just a kid. In my early-twenties at the time, the boss's nephew – and a "college kid" at that. How would all those hardened restaurant veterans feel about me coming in to fill Bernard's bigger than life shoes? And what would I do? What could *anyone* do to try and replace the force of nature that was my "internationally famous" uncle?

Still, I wasn't going to let Bernard or my dad down, and said "yes" as soon as I finally came to my senses. I was a "Fischer Man," after all. Hadn't Bernard's brothers all pitched in, physically and financially, to keep his dream of Bernard's Surf alive, even in those earliest, lean years? The least I could do as his nephew was fill in for a few months until he got back on his feet.

The only problem was, I wasn't sure how Mr. Wickham might take it. After all, he'd personally saved out one of his prime summer spots for me that year and I didn't want to let the man who had been so good to me down. But when he heard the situation and that it was for family, let alone the family business, Joe Wickham waved me off with a grin and said he more than understood.

But working at the Surf turned out to be much more than a summer job. Dad had asked me to stick around for up to a year, which would certainly put a dent in my college career. He assured me I could go back to FSU the following year, and I figured that would be that. I'd pick up with my studies, do the family a favor and graduate a year later than I had expected. Big whoop.

I officially started working at the Surf in May of 1965. Back then the restaurant was one big rectangle at 2 South Atlantic Avenue, on the corner of Minuteman Causeway and A1A.

Then as now, the main door to the bar faced the beach side. When you first walked in, chances are longtime bartender Stan Gardner or his partner Roland Driscoll would greet you as if you were a longtime regular, whether you'd walked in 101 times or this was your very first visit. Behind them hung the famous "Surf Lady" painting, a classy semi-nude that hung over the bar for as long as I can remember – and most folks seeing it for the first time will never forget!

Legend had it that Bernard had won the "naked lady" painting in a poker match and promptly put his "fine art" on display for one and all to see. Most children see their first naked lady in the pages of *National Geographic* magazine. All I had to do was walk into my uncle's bar!

Creaky red leather bar stools would more than likely be filled with regulars who enjoyed the banter of bartender and customer alike. But they were friendly types and would be more than happy to lean to one side if you wanted to reach in between them and order a drink for yourself during those frequent times when the bar cocktail lounge was standing room only. A few booths and tables lined the walls if you wanted a more intimate cocktail hour or something from the limited bar menu.

Drink prices were cheap. Thanks to the space program and Bernard's creative mind, most drink specials featured rocket, spaceship or planet names, like the "Polaris" or "The Atlas". (Much more on these drinks, and how they came to be, later in the book!)

If you were in the mood for more than just a drink and snacks, we had the "Black Room," which was for more casual dining – although still far from what we now know as "casual." Just beyond the Black Room – past another entrance, the bathrooms and of course a cigarette machine – lay the famous Red Room, for more formal affairs and befitting the massive menu that was handed to each guest by one of our formal hostesses.

Behind the bar/lounge area was a small package store, where customers could pick up a pint or two of their favorite beverage on the way home, either from dinner at the Surf or just from work. Either way, Bernard had created a one-stop entertainment complex, part bar, part store, part meal and part show.

So this was Bernard's Surf at the time: a thriving local hot spot, an "internationally famous" destination for four-star cuisine in the heart of the Space Coast. It was where the locals came and the tourists *had* to come, whether they lived in town or were just visiting for the first time.

And starting first thing Monday morning, I'd be learning the ropes. I didn't know whether to laugh or cry, so I just got a good night's sleep, ate my Wheaties the next morning and showed up for duty:

Continuing the Surf Tradition, One Meal at a Time

Talk about your humble beginnings: it was 1965, I was about to turn all of 22-years-old and I was little more than a flunky at the time I started working at Bernard's Surf. But there I was, and no matter how many years as a restaurateur I have left in me, I know that I will never forget my first duty: making tartar sauce.

At that time, we didn't have a mixer, so the Surf used a manual device for the job: my hand and arm! It was a highly complex task: reaching into a 30-gallon container, thoroughly mixing all the ingredients, and transferring the contents to gallon jars to be divvied up into individual portions later on.

Though my first station was "officially" the salad room, where in addition to making tartar sauce I also shredded tons of cabbage for our famous coleslaw or dished up half-and-half salad (half shrimp salad, half crab salad) in fresh carved avocado "bowls," I was more of a jack of all trades than anything else. One night I'd be washing dishes, the next bussing tables or counting steaks or peeling shrimp or mounds of potatoes or onions. There is probably no better way to learn the restaurant business than from the "kitchen up," so I suppose, in a way, it was the best training I could have had. But it sure didn't feel so great heading home smelling like tartar sauce or dishwater after closing the place up every night!

It was a small but efficient organization back then. Meals were long and involved and carefully orchestrated. It could take an hour or two before a table would turn over and new guests could be ushered in. There were cocktails, served up by longtime bartenders Stan and Roland and brought to the table by a real, live cocktail waitress.

There were appetizers to savor and relish trays to sample and bread baskets to plunder and complimentary fried mullet to nibble on and a salad course, more cocktails, naturally, then the actual entree and usually dessert and, of course, "kiddy bags" and Shirley Temples (7-Up and grenadine garnished with maraschino cherries) for the children.

I don't believe we started using the trademark black waitress uniforms with their bright red collars until the early 70s, but even back in the mid-60s when I started at the Surf, everyone "on the floor" dressed up for the occasion, including many of the guests.

It was a different time, a heady time. You could feel the electricity, the excitement, in the air, and definitely in the crowds that came through the Surf's door, eager to be a part of what was eventually to be known as "the space boom".

In the early 1960s President John F. Kennedy had issued his challenge that America should, and would, put a man on the moon. The pace at Cape Canaveral picked up accordingly and, as one of only a handful of restaurants open on the Space Coast at the time, the Surf was front and center for the flurry of activity that followed during the space program in the 60s and 70s.

By the time I started at the Surf in the mid-60s, the space program was in full bloom and in those days of the early Mercury, Gemini and Apollo programs, launches were big affairs. As the Space Center began its three-phase approach to landing a man on the moon, the Space Coast seemed to double, even triple, in occupancy with each new launch.

While always busy, the lounge and bar areas would swell with tourists in town for a launch, as well as national media and the occasional higher up from the space program and even astronauts themselves (more on that later, too).

Others came to the area for a visit, and never left. Many became regular customers, and as I warmed to my duties as a Surf employee I quickly rose through the ranks. Soon I could be trusted to open, then close, the restaurant and management wasn't far off.

With Lou busy with his fishing fleet and Bernard's health unfortunately continuing to fail, I was often left to my own devices in the family restaurant. While it wasn't too hard to figure out how to peel a shrimp, shuck an oyster or shred a head of cabbage, managing a couple dozen employees and learning how to provide hundreds of customers a night with a quality dining experience that would keep them coming back for more – and bringing their friends along – would require a little more effort and expertise.

Chapter 4:

It Takes a Village to Raise a Restaurateur

While every meal seemed to be a learning experience and every customer a crash course in service, hospitality or how to handle complaints, I credit a variety of critical Surf employees those first few years as my unofficial mentors.

Stan Gardner, who worked behind the bar for what seemed like forever and was there when I started working at the Surf and still there for many, many years after, taught me what it meant to cater to new and regular customers alike. Always ready with a smile and an expertly crafted cocktail, Stan was a steady and calming presence when things got tough or busy – or both.

He knew how to read his audience. Stan could lend an ear if a patron wanted to bend more than his elbow, or pour a quick draft and be on his way if someone was just in for a fast lunch and wanted to read their paper over a slice of fresh grouper or skirt steak without being bothered.

He had a flawless work ethic and helped to keep things on an even keel during launches, holidays and other special events where crowd control was just as important as quality control. Having been a long timer even before I got there, Stan knew how things were supposed to work and gently reminded me when they weren't working as well as I thought!

Roland Driscoll shared bartending duties with Stan and together these two loyal Surf veterans helped me to feel more and more confident behind the bar with each shift we worked together.

Between the two of them, Stan and Roland taught me how to bartend with both hands. That's because when I was working a shift with one of them, I had to use my right and, when I was bartending with the other, I'd have to use my left. I can't tell you how handy this simple skill has come in over the years!

Bob Morin worked in the package store but, more importantly, was a constant source of guidance that went well beyond his pay grade or job description. I recall him as a consummate politician, not because he had any grand aspirations to run for office himself, but because he helped me understand the internal and external politics of running a restaurant in a small beachside community such as ours.

Whether it was a petty squabble between waitresses over tips or a power play behind the lines in the kitchen, Bob could help me put my emotions on the back burner and see the forest for the trees to make the right decision for the right dilemma.

Still in my early- to mid-20s by the time I became a manager at the Surf, my life experience was mostly limited to hanging out with my friends and then hanging out with my friends some more. Hardly the type of hard won understanding it took to live up to Bernard's exacting and professional standards.

While I felt I had a good grasp on common sense, I could occasionally be naïve to the hidden agendas of employees, other managers, even customers and guests. Then, as now, there are always those in the workforce looking to "get one over" on those they consider less experienced, or even less confrontational, than themselves. Bob helped me recognize my strengths and weaknesses and use them to my best advantage so that the restaurant always came out on top.

He was also politically savvy when it came to the matters of local ordinances, votes and rulings that might affect the Surf. He could help me see both sides of any issue in the community and clued me in on various decisions to make when it came to voting on a variety of issues that could either hurt or help the Surf's business, or even the community of Cocoa Beach in general.

I still fondly recall our various talks over the sales counter in the package store, or in a quiet booth in the "black room" as Bob ate his lunch or dinner, all the while spoon-feeding a young novice his many years of wisdom and experience.

He was also, along with my father Lou, one of the first people to encourage me to get involved in civic and industry organizations, like the local Chamber of Commerce, Rotary clubs and hotel, lodging and restaurant organizations such as the Florida Restaurant and Lodging

Association, or FRLA, something I continue to do to this day. (As does my youngest son and business partner, Rhett.)

Meeting and greeting other local businesspeople helped me think of the Surf as not just another stand-alone business, but a part of a larger community and one with unlimited growth potential. It helped me see the power of partnerships and the importance of trust in a small but growing, tight knit group of local business owners.

It also kept me plugged into the comings and goings of Brevard's movers and shakers, allowing me to network in ways that would have been impossible if I'd just stuck to my perimeter and never ventured much farther than 2 South Atlantic Avenue.

Ana Mae Petit may have worked in the office, but she provided more than just accounting and bookkeeping skills to a new employee looking to collect more than a paycheck. The Surf was a family business in more than name alone, and folks like Stan, Bob and Ana Mae were part of that family as well.

While Stan and Bob were firm but fair in their mentorship, Ana Mae was more of a mother figure to me. Having lost my own mother at a very young age, I was probably pretty ready for a little motherly advice by the time I started working at the Surf, and with a full staff of cashiers, hostesses and waitresses, I had more than my share of strong, savvy women to guide me on my way.

Not that there was a lot of time for handholding or back pats in those early days. It was tough work in a fast-paced, high-volume restaurant, and lessons came fast and furious, especially to a twenty-something kid trying to learn the ropes in a trial by fire, but Ana Mae was always there with a kind word or gentle suggestion, a nod or a nudge or a reminder or a lesson.

Manning the phones in the office, she could guide me through how to deal with everything from pushy liquor salesmen to waitresses calling in sick at the last minute to how to handle creditors and loan officers at the local bank.

Like a one-two punch of mentorship, Norma Shroble was another early mentor who first worked with Ana Mae in the office and later became a hostess out on the restaurant floor. Norma was perfectly suited for her new job because she was both efficient and joyful about her work.

She could please a regular just by showing them to their favorite table without having to be reminded which one it was or diffuse a tense situation during a long wait with a joke, smirk, smile or witty one-liner.

Equal parts babysitter, taskmaster and permanent "Employee of the Month," Norma became more than a hostess and like an unofficial den mother to everyone at the Surf, its future owner included.

Through her strong and constant presence manning the Surf's front door, Norma schooled patrons and wait staff alike in how to behave in a restaurant!

She was fiercely loyal and energetically tireless and never too busy to teach me a lesson, even while laughing at the way I'd messed something up or occasionally even gotten it half-right – if only by accident! And she was never more vocal than when praising me for a job well done, even if that happened less frequently than I would have liked back in those days.

The restaurant business is a unique universe and anyone who's ever worked in one, which would have to be half of the Space Coast I would imagine, knows that unique and special person who makes a tough shift easier and an easy shift a night to remember.

For as long as I could remember, Norma *was* that presence at Bernard's Surf. Night after night, year after year, from a few years before I started at the Surf to well into the 80s, she steered us all through countless busy nights and would-be catastrophes and, in the process, helped me become a better leader in my own right.

Norma's kids worked for us too, off and on over the years: her daughters, Patti as a cashier and Juli as waitresses and her husband, Pete, as a bartender. Her son Mark worked as a busboy and in the salad room and Charlie was a last-minute dishwasher when needed. In fact, if you're enjoying even a few of the pictures in this book, and more than a few of the memories, you can thank Juli Shroble for a lot of them!

Not every mentor I had during those early years worked at the Surf. Eli Weismann, the baker who played such a big role in my prom night by saving Bernard's butt with a last-minute order of pumpernickel rolls, was not only a local vendor but a mentor and, eventually, a friend.

Eli did all our baking, from the pumpernickel rolls with fresh onions inside to the onion board that was such a highlight of our world famous breadbasket, and a fond memory for thousands of customers over the years.

From Bernard's time to now my time, I was fortunate to "inherit" a colleague like Eli, who was as dependable as he was friendly and accommodating.

And like so many of the people I've dealt with over the years, from employees to vendors to customers, over the years Eli became a friend. We always hired him to make a cake for Rusty Jr. on his birthday, and I'll never forget the year he took every toy in the bakery and put them on Rusty's three-tiered cake.

I think that was the last of the over-the-top cakes we ever requested, but it was a hard one to forget and I can't imagine any other baker in town going to the same kind of trouble for a five-year-old!

But it's moments like that, when people enter into your family occasions, or when they come to celebrate theirs at your restaurant, when you get a glimpse of them as more than just people or employees or customers, but as an almost surrogate family member. There would be many more over the years to come, but Eli was one of the first.

Brushfires, Misfires and Wrong Hires

As a young restaurateur in training in the mid-60s, it was only natural I'd be a magnet for friends and family looking to get into – or as the case might be after a few chaotic night shifts, out of – the restaurant business.

For those who don't know any better, it seems like the perfect spot to spend a few hours a night, deliver a few drinks, wash a few dishes, make a few salads, collect your tips and go home with a pocket full of cold, hard cash.

Easy money for easy work, or so it would seem. Once they've been hit with a two-hour wait on a busy Saturday night, though, the truth becomes plain, and many can't stand the heat and get out before ever having to endure another shift in the restaurant industry.

My old pal Bruce Arrow was one of the first to hit me up for a job once word spread that I was "in like Flynn" at the Surf. I put him to work in the salad room and had to remind him every so often that,

43

yes, we were friends but that I was also, technically speaking, his boss. Come to think of it, I had to remind him of that on a daily basis.

My brother Ronnie also signed up for a tour of Surf duty and was soon toiling away in the salad room as well. I'm not sure whether it was too much of a good thing or not enough, but either way it was doomed from the start.

Neither Bruce nor Ronnie was very suited to the restaurant business, I'm afraid, especially *my* restaurant business. The fur really flew when I found out they'd been keeping the bar open after hours to fuel their addictions to wine, women and song, and ultimately I fired both in short succession. We laugh about it now, but it wasn't so funny when I quickly had to find replacements for them on the fly.

It was also a painful lesson in learning how to cope with friends and family in a business relationship, and helped me to separate the professional from the personal, as I'd have to do with increasing regularity in later years. And, of course, it was all for the best.

Ronnie went on to great success while working with Dad in the seafood business, leading to a long and fulfilling career that seemed better suited to his particular skill set. And Bruce went on to graduate from FSU before dominating the world of insurance, meeting his beautiful wife Marilee along the way.

And I stayed behind, trying to steer the Surf in the right direction and hold down the fort until Bernard's health improved and he could return to the Surf and send me back to school.

A Permanent Position

So much happened from the spring of 1965, when I first started working at Bernard's Surf, to the fall of that same year that it almost seemed to happen overnight, or at least flew by in a blur.

One morning I'd shown up for work, been handed an apron and a timecard and shoved into the claustrophobic salad room and the next I was walking into work in a suit and tie, ready for another day managing my uncle's restaurant in his absence.

That's when disaster struck, personally *and* professionally. Bernard died suddenly in October of 1965 and in the aftermath, when we were all finally able to take a breath from the shock of it all, my father came to me with an ultimatum: I could go back to college and pick up my old life, as promised, or I could stay on at the Surf and, eventually, take it over.

It was a game changing decision for a young man at a literal crossroads in his life. Going back to being a part-time college student, with all the temptations that life entailed, versus becoming a full-time business *owner*. Frat parties and beer kegs or employee disputes and the dishwasher breaking down in the middle of a Saturday night rush.

Once upon a time, the choice would have been clear enough: hit the road and get back to a regular life, like my brother Ronnie had and Bruce Arrow along with him, to say nothing of my good friends Bill and Kim Hammond and most everyone else I'd gone to school with at Melbourne High only a few short years earlier. But now things were different.

I had gotten married over the summer and was starting to make the kinds of decisions husbands made, not frat boys. I knew I had to start thinking about settling down soon, but... *this* soon?

For that matter, what *did* I want from my life?

What did the future hold, and what did I want it to look like?

Was I ready to own a restaurant?

And did I even *want* to?

Would I have time for my new bride, and the children we hoped to have together, working six days a week at the Surf, and being on call 24-hours a day, 365 days a year?

These were just some of the questions that ran through my mind as Bernard's death sank in and my father's ultimatum finally registered. Surprisingly, it didn't take me as long as I thought it might to decide. Although I'd never consciously set out to join the family business, I found myself distressed at the thought of having to leave it now that I'd been indoctrinated in such a powerful and intense way over the previous year.

I'd been through so much in those few short months I'd worked at the Surf, and had achieved even more, that the thought of returning to college and sitting in a classroom only to start over after graduation at someone else's business no longer seemed very attractive to me.

I told Dad I'd "think about it," but secretly I knew my answer before I was driving away from Dad's condo on the beach. The Surf was more than just a restaurant; to me, to my family, to the community. I couldn't just turn my back on that responsibility now that I'd seen how important it was to the lives of so many local residents.

And I wouldn't. And, ultimately, I didn't. The very next day I told Dad I was up for the challenge and, after doing so, I think we both felt relieved. It was only later, when the dust settled and the adrenaline subsided that I realized just what I was in for.

And even then, I didn't know the half of it:

Chapter 5:

Defining Moments

A s the swinging 60s rolled on toward the politically turbulent 70s, I rolled up my sleeves and continued to try and steer the Surf through the changing times and broadening horizons that the politics and passion of the era provided.

With the space program in full swing and the town of Cocoa Beach front and center for all the action, on the launch pads and in the sunny blue skies overhead, it was a heady and hopeful time for all involved. It was also a fragile time, as anyone who has ever tried to build a brand and steer a business in the right direction can tell you.

A Legacy in the Making

It was also a time of great change, both personally and professionally. The Fischer Men, in particular, didn't fare too well as the 1960s finally came to a close. By 1965 Bernard was gone and his brother and business partner, Sidney, was soon to follow.

Sidney Fischer, who had once been the mayor of Cocoa Beach and a driving force on the local political scene, died in 1968 after a prolonged illness. With Sidney's passing, I couldn't help but think that another era was ending as well.

He and Bernard had always been such a great team, be it manning the bar at the Surf or immersing themselves in community affairs and local politics. And why not? They'd been a part of the Cocoa Beach Community since the Surf opened in 1948.

When folks moved into town, the first – and only – place for them to "whet their whistle" was the Surf. It was also the closest place to pick up a pint of booze or a piece of gossip or a nugget of good advice about where to live or find a good, steady job. This was old school

Cocoa Beach, old school America, where you could trust a working man and they could trust you.

During various construction projects on and around Patrick Air Force Base in the early 50s or so, I believe, the construction workers would come to Bernard's package store to cash their checks since so few of them had bank accounts, or were willing to open one. Worker after worker would come to cash their check, and stay for a little more.

Of course, Sidney, who ran the package store then, would make them buy something for the privilege so they'd naturally pick up a pint of vodka or rum to jump start the transaction. Well, every so often Sidney would have to run out to the bank, deposit all these checks, get more cash, come back and cash more checks.

But it wasn't just the locals. I can't tell you how many times someone had just moved into town, needed cash to pay the movers and, hearing of his generosity, would come up to the Surf and watch Bernard cash their check so they could pay the mover or put a deposit down or whatever was the case. So from the very start, the Surf and the Fischer Men had been about building the Space Coast, regardless of personal cost. And now their legacy was about to change hands.

Bernard died at 45, then Sidney passed away in his early 60s. A third brother, Eddie, helped Dad with the seafood business, and had a few stores in downtown Cocoa in the 1940s and 50s. One sold seafood and another dry goods.

I remember Eddie telling me that Sundays were "dry" in Brevard County back in the day, meaning you couldn't sell alcohol. But his customers still wanted a little hooch with their fresh seafood. Or, in most cases, just the booze! So ingeniously, Eddie would sell them overpriced trout or flounder and slip a pint of something extra in the bag with the fish.

But after Eddie passed away, my father, Lou, was the only Fischer brother remaining. If anyone could steer the Fischer legacy, it was Dad. Strong and stable with a good head for business, he inspired me to run the Surf the same way he'd run his own successful businesses over the years.

What's more, he reminded me that if the Fischer name was to go on, my brother Ronnie and I would be responsible for doing just that.

Ronnie fulfilled his part by running the Miss Cape Canaveral out of Port Canaveral (in a building that would soon house the off shoot of a later Surf venture, Rusty's Seafood and Oyster Bar!).

While I'd crewed the Miss Charleston one summer in the early 60s, Ronnie ran the show full-time and, just like our father, made fishing his business. (Which was a good thing, seeing as I'd recently suggested that he "move on" from the restaurant business!)

Defining Moments

There is a difference between managing a restaurant and owning one. It was a difference I would have to discover, and master, for myself. Despite Bernard's legacy and all he'd done for the restaurant he first started, and never stopped believing in, I never had the opportunity to learn much from him, personally.

It would have been nice to learn from the master himself, but by the time I arrived on the scene, Bernard's health was failing and I was pretty much left to find my own way, and on my own terms. Maybe, in a sense, it was better this way. Lessons taught are not always learned, and experience can often be the best teacher. Then, too, there was no shortage of teachers willing to lend the latest "Fischer Man" their years of expertise or patient guidance. That is, if he was willing to soak up all that knowledge they'd gained.

Thanks to employees turned mentors like Stan and Bob and Ana Mae and Norma, I was well on my way to learning my own style of leadership, but clearly I still had a lot to learn… and spent much of the 60s and 70s, and my own 20s and 30s, doing just that.

One defining moment in my ownership of the restaurant that truly stands out came when I was forced to reprimand a cocktail waitress named, oddly enough, "Rusty". It was the late 60s, early 70s, and by then I'd known Rusty since my teens, when Bernard's son Jerry and I would go to her house and hangout and eat ice cream and generally goof off.

This was back in the day when the Surf, when many restaurants in fact, still had cocktail waitresses. You don't see them much anymore, but back then the cocktail waitress did just that: took the cocktail orders – and only the cocktail orders – and brought the drinks. Then, like a good tag team, the regular waitress took the dinner order. At the end of the night, they split the tips down the middle.

At least, that's how it was supposed to work. This one night in question, however, Rusty got greedy. I can't remember what exactly the circumstances were, but I remember her getting in one of my server's faces and maybe demanding more money than she was actually owed. Whatever the case, it was either brought to my attention or just didn't feel right and I knew something had to be done. And that night, I was the only one around who could do something about it.

There were two bathrooms in a little alcove between the Red Room and the Black Room, with a wall separating them from the restaurant proper. I can remember yanking Rusty back into the darkened alcove and reading her the riot act. Specifically I stuck my finger in her face and told her if she ever did that again, she wouldn't have a job at the Surf anymore.

I didn't know how she'd react. Heck, I didn't even know how I'd react. I didn't have time to anticipate a reaction, or even really care, at that point. Instinct took over and, for better or worse, led me to reprimand her in my own, unique, personal style. I waited with bated breath for her to react in some way: shout back, blame, accuse, cry, storm off, something. But this is what she finally said after I'd given her my ultimatum: "Yes, sir."

For me, it was a defining moment because we had suddenly and forever crossed over from that friendly relationship we used to have, and merged into a professional one. We'd gone from mutual friends to employee and boss, and what's more, others knew what was going on, had heard it, seen inklings of it, or the aftermath or just the momentarily ugly vibe of a boss reprimanding an employee just out of earshot.

I know it must have been a shock for her, hearing an order from this "kid" she used to make ice cream sundaes for at her house, who was now her boss. But for me, it was just one of many "friendly" confrontations I'd be forced to make over the years as the restaurant, and my confidence, grew. But believe it or not, there weren't as many such ugly moments as one might think.

For one, I eventually learned to hire people to deal with that kind of thing for me, and for another I tried to hire the right people, family people, the first time around so that we didn't have to have those kinds of confrontations in the first place.

Rusty probably walked away from that incident with a new respect for her boss, and I guess I did, too! It wouldn't be the last time I had to assert myself in a leadership role, but it was certainly one of the first and, for me, one of the most memorable.

And Rusty and I were fine after that. We had our moment, we understood our roles and how to play them and we moved on. Like many of the people who worked at the Surf, she was more friend, even family member, than employee. I can vividly remember her spending an evening at our house, playing with our boys years later, so I guess it's true that all's well that ends well.

For me, the moment helped me become more demonstrative in the way I managed, even led, a very diverse and adult crew. It also made me realize that in order to lead, I would need a good manager to play interference.

Unfortunately, my search in that department continued.

Without Checks and Balances, You're Signing a Blank Check

I was a lot more innocent back then than I am today. I'll never forget the look on Rusty Junior's face as he was sitting in my office, many years later, as I handled a routine liquor order. He'd stopped by for something, probably to ask for money or a favor, as I recall (!), and was sitting across from my desk as I handled the call. For me, it was strictly routine, another day on the job, not even a blip on my daily radar, but for "Junior Rusty" – as my grandson Jack calls him – it was quite an eye opener!

When I got off the phone he looked a little frustrated, maybe even disappointed, with me. "What?" I asked.

"You were kind of rude to that guy, weren't you?"

"Was I?" I asked, but before he could answer I reminded him, "Well, you could only hear my half of the conversation. If you'd been able to hear all the stupid deals he was offering me, you'd have cut him off, too."

"Still…" he said, not entirely convinced. "You were pretty rude."

"Sometimes, Russ, you need to be blunt in this business. To you,

51

that might sound 'rude'. To someone who's trying to sell me something I don't need, that sounds like their cue to sell me something I *do*."

And in this case, I was right. The salesman had been young, inexperienced and just trying to make a quick buck by unloading a bunch of liquor I'd never use, at prices they were hardly worth. I'm not sure Rusty Jr. got it back then, but I think he trusted me enough to know that I wasn't being rude just to be rude.

The fact is, you have to have a kind of hard exterior in this business or folks will rip you off, as often – and for as much as – they can. I learned that the hard way during that first year or two at the Surf, and was often reminded of that lesson throughout my 60-plus years tenure as a restaurateur.

Case in point: at some point in those first few years, I hadn't quite mastered the art of monitoring my people to a science. Between the transition from Bernard running the place to me trying to pick up his slack, some wires got crossed and our system of checks and balances wasn't at its strongest, so to speak.

When you don't have enough pairs of eyes on one department or another, savvy folks with an opportunistic eye will quickly swoop in to take advantage of the lapse in security. When those folks are in charge of counting your money, troubles can mount fast, but not quite as fast as the money goes missing!

We had a cashier in those days, who at this point will remain anonymous for obvious reasons! Well, she not only counted the money at night, but counted it again in the morning. Like I said, no checks, no balances, and someone savvy is going to step in and put a hand in the till. It's simply human nature.

Well, that's just what she did. Every night she'd take a little from the count, then in the morning she'd take a little more, and since she was tallying both figures, no one else in the organization was any the wiser to the double sums of missing money. Twenty dollars here, thirty dollars there, twice a day, five or six days a week, and her bank account was growing fatter while ours was growing thinner.

She'd just write a new figure that balanced out and since it looked good on paper, that was good enough for me. I just thought business was off, which felt a little funny since we were busier than ever. That was probably how she got away with it for so long. The busier we were, the longer my nights lasted, and the earlier my mornings, the more money she had to play around with as she cooked the books and lined her own pocketbook without anyone, least of all me, looking over her shoulder to make sure the figures she tallied were correct.

By the time we finally got wise and started paying a little closer attention to the books, well, our night/day cashier had helped herself to the tune of a whopping $10,000!

Cocoa Beach is still considered a small town now, and believe me when I tell you it was much, *much* smaller way back then. We called the cashier and her husband in, because we knew them both quite well, and showed her the "evidence." She admitted it, tearfully as I recall, and her husband agreed to reimburse us for the ten grand rather than watch his wife be taken off to jail.

I wish I could say that was the first, and last, time an employee ripped me off, but that would make this book a novel and not non-fiction! Now, you'd think being burned once would have taught us a thing or two about who counted our money, but remember: the learning curve may be steep in the restaurant business, but it's still a curve.

Eventually there was another busy season in the restaurant business, another new bookkeeper, and another new opportunity for money to go "missing" from right under our nose. Well, in our new system, rather than letting the morning cashier go make the bank deposit every morning, we decided to have our new bookkeeper at the time do it instead.

Well, somehow this new bookkeeper found a way to not only manipulate the deposit to reflect an amount that was less than correct, but to write a check for the difference – a check to herself.

I may have never found out about it, or perhaps would only have found out about it another $10,000 later, if the assistant bookkeeper hadn't called me at the Surf one Saturday morning, flustered and upset, to let me know what she'd figured out.

She said, "Rusty, I'm sorry to bother you but I'm upset and I have to get this off my chest, but… she [the accountant] is depositing less than the full amount and writing herself a check for the difference."

Well, by this time, I had decided in my young career that enough was enough. Why should I keep turning the other cheek when all anybody else was doing was slapping it silly? Rather than reaching out to the bookkeeper and trying to handle it without alerting the authorities, like I had in the past, this time I just picked up the phone and called the police.

Apparently she was getting her hair done at a local salon when the cops went to arrest her. I got a call from the Cocoa Beach Police Department a short while later saying they were taking her to jail. I don't know why, but I asked them to make sure to drive by the restaurant on the way.

The deputy said they would and I walked outside the bar to wait. Sure enough, a few minutes later they drove by, turning left from Minutemen Causeway and onto A1A. Our former bookkeeper was in the backseat, blond hair recently done, head down in shame as they drove past her place of employment on the way to parts, and a future, unknown.

I think part of that drive past the Surf was to show her I knew what she'd done and wasn't going to let her get away with stealing from me. I think part of it was pride that while I had just lost one distrustful employee, I had realized that the assistant bookkeeper who called me cared enough about her job, our restaurant and myself to turn her co-worker in. Also, more than a little, it was a silent message to others who might be thinking about ripping me off: if you try, be prepared to pay the consequences.

Beware the Milk Man

All of which brings us to another case in the ongoing files of a new restaurant owner learning the ropes in his family business: the Case of the Mischievous Milkman. By this point I'd graduated to counting the steaks each morning. It might not sound like a big deal but, for a guy who'd been washing dishes and bussing tables for six or seven months straight, it was definitely a promotion.

Well, on this particular morning I'd counted the steaks and tallied the numbers and made sure that Bo Pete, our butcher extraordinaire, knew just how many filets, sirloins, porterhouses and chops to prepare for the lunch and dinner shifts that day.

We went through so much milk in the Surf that gallon jugs just wouldn't do, so we had a cooler about the size of large rectangular suitcase that dispensed milk by the glassful. The milk came in giant plastic bags, housed in boxes to keep them upright so they'd fit conveniently into the cooler. At one end of the bag was a little white tube, or spigot, and you snipped it off and out came the milk.

Anyway, the milkman delivered them in these big white boxes and, every day, instead of just delivering the boxes he'd actually go into the machine, see if the milk bags were empty and, if so, he'd replace them. As he left he'd usually be carrying at least one or two empty boxes out with him to dispose of in the dumpster outside.

I always thought the guy was just being nice, going above and beyond the call of duty to make sure his customers were happy, but I quickly learned the real reasons for his "generosity" once I'd graduated to counting steaks.

As I was heading out to the floor for something or other one morning, I happened to glance over and spot the milkman leaning into the walk-in cooler before putting his hand in one of the empty milk boxes.

I'm not big into confrontation so I didn't say anything at the time, but the minute he was gone I went inside the cooler and, sure enough, three or four of the steaks I'd just counted were suddenly missing. Armed with proof, I rushed out to the parking lot where his delivery truck was still idling in the side alley next to the restaurant.

I whipped open the front cab only to find an eight- or nine-year-old boy sitting there, waiting patiently for his dad to finish his morning deliveries. It was summer, mid-July, and I figured the kid was just tagging along. Cheaper than a babysitter, right?

But that didn't stop me from shutting the door and heading to the back of the truck, where the milkman was just shutting his cooler. Surprised to see me, he opened his mouth to form a greeting but I never let him.

"First of all," I said, "put the steaks back. Second of all, don't ever deliver to this restaurant again. I'm not gonna call your boss, but obviously he's gonna ask some questions when you can't come back here anymore. But you should have thought of that before you stole my steaks."

I don't know what happened to him after that, or his little boy, but at that moment I frankly didn't care. It was just one more lesson for a new restaurant manager to learn: not only do you have to keep an eye on your staff, but you've got to watch out for the folks who deliver for you as well. Charlie Ragland, who I later hired as my general manager, or GM, likes to tell a similar story where at closing time for a few nights one week, he noticed several of the waitresses heading out of the restaurant with larger than usual purses.

It was the mid-70s or so, and larger purses weren't exactly in style at the time, and plus they seemed to be pretty darn full and the girls seemed quite protective of them as they shuffled off after another busy shift.

One night Charlie blocked the door like a bouncer at a nightclub and said, "All right, girls, I know we're all tired and it's late but, humor me and empty your purses on the bar." (Of course, you'd never get away with that nowadays but, those were different times, so long, long ago.)

The waitresses did as they were told and, as Charlie loved to recall it – I may have heard the story from him more than once!!! – out onto the bar spilled tomatoes, steaks, onions, entire heads of lettuce, rolls, you name it. Suddenly, the top of the bar looked like a full-on buffet!

But in typical Charlie fashion, none of them lost their jobs. (Though they did lose their stash for the night!) Instead he told them, "Girls, I understand when things get tight, trust me. If you NEED something, tell me, I'll give you anything you want. But never steal from me or Rusty again."

He paused for effect and added, in typical Charlie fashion, "And tomorrow night, bring smaller purses!"

More Than Just a Manager

I'd grown up on the business side of things, checks and balances, counting the money, running food costs, signing checks, showing my face on the dining room floor, wearing a three-piece suit.

What I needed now was a foodie type manager, a sergeant at arms, a second in command, someone who knew food and people and how to get the most out of both.

In short, an Operations Guy.

In 1973, I finally found him. I was at a Chamber of Commerce function at the old Piccadilly's Cafeteria in the Merritt Square Mall. A young manager there caught my eye. He was a hustler and a self-starter, fast and proficient, energetic and loud, and before the evening was over I approached him and introduced myself. I also put a bug in his ear that, if he was ever interested in managing Bernard's Surf, to give me a call.

A week or so later, to my surprise, he did just that.

The hiring process took longer than it might have for other positions, say signing on a new waitress or prep cook, but I wanted to be sure hiring my new General Manager would be the right fit. I wanted folks I knew to talk to Charlie before I hired him, and I wanted him to talk to them. Most of all, I wanted us both to be happy, and that included Charlie as well.

For his part, Charlie recalls walking through the Surf on his first official "visit" behind the scenes and seeing a lot of potential. Though he never said anything to me at the time, he spent most of his tour spotting a prospective – or glaring – problem and thinking, "Oh, I could fix that! Oh, wow, that really needs work. Oh, I have a solution for that…"

So maybe Charlie accepted the job as more of a personal challenge, to see how quickly, and successfully, he could turn the kitchen, the staff, the meal prep and time to table around. Maybe it was more of a personal challenge for Charlie than a personal connection between the two of us, but I like to think it was a little bit of both.

Swing Shifts and Slick Ties

Part of my job, first as a manager at the Surf and later, as the owner, was to walk the dining room floor during the restaurant's busiest shifts. That meant going table to table, putting hands on shoulders and making eye contact and asking everyone how their meal was. I enjoyed it more as the years went on, but it was hard at first and never felt entirely comfortable.

I was happier behind the bar, where I could wash glasses and crack open beers and uncork wine bottles and pour two fingers of a regular's favorite cocktail. In a way, I'm still most comfortable behind the bar and when things get busy and it's "all hands on deck," it's the first place I tend to gravitate.

I always made it a point to wear a tie to work back in those days and, like most guys who went to work during the 60s and 70s, I had some doozies. I don't wear a tie to work anymore but, to this day, my children still remind me of some of the more "colorful" ones.

Different Times, Same Restaurant

Part of continuing the Surf's rich and storied legacy was honoring old traditions that guests had come to know and love over the years, all the while starting new ones that would hopefully stand the test of time. Many of you might recall the more "exotic" items on the Surf menu over the years, and reading through them as I write this chapter makes me glad the Surf was never on PETA's radar back in the 50s and 60s!

Mexican iguana, buffalo and kangaroo steaks, fried grasshoppers, roasted caterpillars and chocolate covered bees, these were just a few of the choice, no doubt now illegal items that Bernard had served with pride over the years.

Some of these items were in the service of creating a diverse and "international" menu, something Bernard was keenly interested in doing as more and more foreign engineers and (literal) rocket scientists visited the area to work for the Space Program. But a lot of it was just plain marketing. "Exotic Specialties from Far Off Lands," he called them, on and off the menu, and rightfully so. Bernard knew that if folks saw something like "Fried Agave Worms from Mexico" or "Kangaroo Tail Soup from Australia" on the menu, they'd be sure to tell their friends, and their friends would tell their friends.

We might not have served a ton of those exotic menu items on a daily basis, if ever, but they sure created a buzz, as well as a lasting impression, and when it comes to marketing your restaurant, I suppose that's half the battle.

As times and tastes changed over the years, we eventually phased out our more exotic items and turned our attention to what the Surf was really known for: quality food and service on par with five-star restaurants all over the world.

Bernard was proud of being able to call his restaurant "internationally known," and for good reason. So many of the engineers who worked on or for the space program were from Germany or France or all over the globe, and when they would go home and tell their friends about the great dinners they'd had at the Surf well, there we were: internationally known.

Again, there was just enough truth in the bold claim to make it technically accurate and that gave Bernard the green light to print it on the menu, and anywhere else he could. Again, Marketing 101; it just seemed to come naturally to Bernard.

Back when I took over the Surf and for many years afterward, Cocoa Beach was a fun, popular, thriving place to live, work and play. It was flush with space program money, and busy with smart and talented people who worked hard but also played hard. After a long week, or just another long day, they liked to unwind with a few cocktails and a nice dinner and let their hair down.

Back then, dinner was still an event. Folks dressed up, listened to music, had cocktails and hors d'oeuvres, maybe even got up and danced, and gave themselves a few hours to enjoy the experience. Weeknights or weekends, it was just what people did. And as Cocoa Beach grew, there seemed to be more and more places for them to do it!

Our strongest competition back then was Ramon's, the famous and respected eatery folks still talk about to this day. Prime rib, their famous Caesar salad served with a homemade – and secret – dressing recipe, generous portions and great service.

Old timers will remember Ramon's near the corner of 520 and A1A, a two-story building that was the site of many family dinners and celebrations. Nolan's Pub is there now, in a new strip mall built on the lot where the old building once stood.

Those golden years of dancing, drinking and dining on the growing Space Coast also featured the Mouse Trap, just past the Cape Canaveral Pier and featuring the same kind of cocktail lounge and dinner atmosphere as Ramon's and the Surf.

George's Steakhouse was another popular eatery locals may or may not remember. It sat just north of the Golf N Gator putt-putt course. There's a Dollar General there now, but I can still remember the restaurant in its prime, its parking lot full of admiring fans and its dining room full of satisfied customers.

Dad and I still leased the property on which the Surf sat from Mr. Casbon, who was a barber by trade but a shrewd businessman by nature. As a rule, I never let his humble appearance or small barber shop fool me. After all, the man had built the Surf when Cocoa Beach was just a bunch of soft sand and scrub brush and, by now, he owned half of the downtown area!

Fortunately for us, he still owned the Surf as well. I believe we only paid him $458 in rent each month back in the day, but the fact was it was still his building and the Surf was having growing pains as it, and the bustling town around it, grew older by the day.

It was the 70s by now and I was building some new offices on the land we owned next to the Surf, and Dad and I both thought it was time we bought the building outright from its rightful owner.

So I went next door to the barber shop and said, "Mr. Casbon, I'm starting this new building and it'd probably be better if I owned the Surf outright, so… I'd like to buy it."

He thought for a minute and said, "You know, son, if I sell it to you, I'm going to have to pay a lot in taxes, and you're going to have to pay me a lot more money, so why don't we both make our lives easier and keep it the way it is right now."

And me being the master negotiator I am, I said, "Well, okay, if that's what you want."

Not long after that fateful meeting, Mr. Casbon passed away. Eventually, his son and fellow FSU alumni, John Casbon, and I finally worked out a deal to buy the land upon which the Surf sat in 1975. Like most of my friends or family at some point, John actually came to work for me for six months or so before deciding the restaurant business wasn't for him. (Now, where have I heard that before?)

In addition to buying the land from the Casbon family, I had bought the restaurant itself from Dad back in 1973. It was eight years after I'd taken over running the place, I was in my early 30s by then and felt it was time to either shift into ownership gear or, as they say, "get off the pot".

While I'd like to take all the credit for this wise business decision, the idea was basically pushed on my father and I by our insurance agent, Tommy Alston.

He basically said, "Lou, why don't you just sell the business to this boy. You're not getting any younger and he's doing a pretty good job and he needs to have an ownership role to keep him around."

I couldn't have said it any better myself, and apparently Dad agreed!

A Tradition in the Making

By 1973 it was official: I owned more than just the Surf restaurant, but the original building where it had opened on Halloween night in 1948. Dad signed the business over to me for a mere $140,000. Although, at the time, there was no "mere" about it; that was still a princely sum to a kid just entering his 30s. But Dad had a good heart, and raised my salary the same amount as the mortgage payment so, in essence, the business paid off the restaurant and I never felt the pinch or pressure of the additional payments on the building in my actual paycheck. The feeling at the time was one of great relief, but also great responsibility.

I'd always felt that the Surf was more than just a restaurant, but an institution. I don't mean that to sound cocky, but for me running the business was always far more than professional and instead deeply, deeply personal.

Not only was I proud of the fact that I was able to employ hardworking family men and women with responsibilities and provide them with a paycheck every week, but I also felt a deeply ingrained sense of responsibility to those who came before me.

Along with the building that housed the Surf, I inherited a boat load of customs, habits, nostalgia, dishes, plates and, above all, regular customers. Many of these I knew already and all, it seemed, were eager to test out the "new guy".

Or, in some cases, just mess with the other customers.

One of these good-natured troublemakers was an old salt named Cliff Heney. Cliff was just one such "regular" I inherited from Bernard, who was fiercely loyal if he liked you, and a right ornery cuss if he didn't. Cliff was as old timer as they got. In fact, he had designed the first business check Bernard ever used for the Bernard's Surf account.

As a long time regular, of course, Cliff had his favorite seat at the bar. There were no reserved seats, of course, but anyone who's ever worked behind a bar – or even sat at one – can tell you that regulars definitely have "their" seats.

Cliff would pull up outside the Surf in his giant Cadillac – and I do mean giant, as only sedans built and sold in the 1960s were giant –

which took up not only "his" parking space but a good portion of A1A as well.

As you can imagine, it wasn't an easy car to park and if he found himself in too tight a spot, no problem. Cliff would simply put the Caddy in reverse and slowly, very slowly, nudge the offending car that was too close to his bumper gently out of the way. (And even less gently if no one was around to witness the act!)

When Cliff was finally satisfied with his parking spot, he'd walk into the lounge and head straight for "his" seat at the bar. It wasn't a great seat, but it was over in the corner, practically behind the beer taps, and apparently it suited Cliff just fine.

After all, he sat there for nearly 30 years!

So if his seat was open – and the other regulars knew to keep it open – he'd plop himself down for a double vodka on the rocks. He only had one, and he'd nurse it all afternoon before heading home for a quick nap before returning to his favorite seat and one more double vodka on the rocks.

From time to time, there were those rare occasions when Cliff's seat wasn't available, in which case he'd find another open seat at the bar, sit himself down and quietly glare at the offending customer until they either got the hint and scooted right away – which was usually the case – or finished their drink and, the minute they'd vacated "his" seat, would quickly scoot himself in, smile and order his drink.

Harry Wagner was another one of my favorite regulars. A veteran's veteran, Harry flew a jaw-dropping 11 sorties during the Normandy invasion on D-Day.

Like Cliff, Harry could be a crusty sort if things didn't go his way, so as often as possible I tried to get them to go his way! But like Cliff, he was an almost daily presence at the Surf, and these older guys livened up the place with their salty humor, war stories, off color jokes and sense of camaraderie.

They were a lot like stubborn, ornery uncles who liked to give you the business but also tried to steer you along in life. Only unlike real stubborn, ornery uncles, who you only saw once or twice a year on holidays, you saw them every day!

Both Cliff and Harry were widowers who, I suppose, had found a second living room seated around the Surf's new circular bar. While

Cliff was a devoted lunch and dinner patron, and had been for years, Harry started a little slower.

He and his wife used to come in on Saturday nights together but, after she passed away, Harry started coming in for lunch almost every day. It was more than just a hot meal he didn't have to cook himself, even I knew that.

Like any regulars, Cliff and Harry were just looking for a little companionship to while away the hours and keep a smile on their faces. Not that either man was the jovial sort, but once you got to know them you realized their bark was a lot worse than their bite and could eventually see the sweetness behind the salty exteriors.

Of course, Cliff and Harry weren't the only traditions I inherited when I took over the Surf. Bernard was a sentimental man, and back in a day when class still mattered, he had it in spades. If he knew a favorite customer was having an anniversary or birthday, he'd stop by the table and give them a gift. It could be a lighter with the Surf logo engraved on it, or a fancy pen or an oddity or some other kitschy item of the day. God love him, but Bernard was a sucker for salesmen.

Guys could come in offering personalized pens or measuring tapes shaped like miniature homes or engraved coffee mugs and he'd always order a batch as giveaways, then keep their card and make special orders for even more special customers.

I guess I had inherited them as well…

Chapter 6:

Florida Today... and Tomorrow

I was saddened to hear of the passing of the legendary Al Neuharth not long ago. While you may or may not know the man's name, you're probably more than familiar with his globe-spanning legacy.

If you've ever read a copy of *USA Today*, or merely had one slipped under your hotel room door while on vacation or a business trip, you can thank Mr. Neuharth, founder of *USA Today*. Of course, those on the Space Coast may be more familiar with one of his first journalistic endeavors, starting *Today* newspaper in Brevard, which he later changed to *Florida Today*.

While it may seem odd to find the name of a globe-trotting media titan play so dominantly in a book about the restaurant business and the Space Coast, the fact is that neither Bernard's Surf nor Brevard County would have been the same without the presence of Al Neuharth.

And, frankly, neither would I...

A Newspaper Man

Neuharth came to Brevard County in the mid-60s, right about the time I was starting in the family business at the Surf. Having worked for the *Miami Herald* early in his journalism career, Neuharth was instrumental in launching *Today* newspaper, revolutionizing the way papers were written, designed and even distributed in Brevard County and, later, all over the country.

He clearly fell in love with the area, and set up "base camp" in a beautiful home right on the ocean at 3rd Street in Cocoa Beach. In honor of his South Dakota roots, he called the house "Pumpkin Center" and it was to be his home office for much of his work, and life, both during the *Florida Today* and *USA Today* eras.

Neuharth spoke often of his love for the Space Program and the Space Coast, in general, and Cocoa Beach, in particular. And not just to me. In an interview for his beloved *Florida Today* newspaper, Neuharth once said of the area, "I thought it was as beautiful as any place in Florida and it was more exciting because you had all these young people and all these space people here."

The Pumpkin Center grew to be a massive residence, with sprawling additions over the years, stately and palatial, something you'd be more likely to see in the Hamptons or Palm Beach than our little seaside town, and was a testimony to Neuharth's obsession with quality and excellence in every area of his life.

It was also located across the street and just a few blocks down from the Surf, making it a natural "go to" spot for Mr. Neuharth. That is, once he found it up to his incredibly high standards, of course.

A Rocky Start

I first met Al under less than auspicious circumstances and, for better or worse, that initial meeting contained many of the benchmarks of how our relationship was going to proceed from that day forward. Al could be a challenging man, demanding and superior, but he was also exceedingly fair and taught me a lot about expecting the best, even on a busy weeknight.

That was a busy night at the Surf, a launch night and as always we were packed to the rafters. Mr. Neuharth – as I referred to him that night and for many years afterward – had reserved a table ahead of time but, for whatever reason, it wasn't quite ready yet when he arrived on the scene. After conferring with everyone else in the chain of command at the Surf that the table he had reserved wasn't actually ready, he finally asked to speak to me.

I knew of him by reputation, of course, and even if I hadn't I would have approached him with deference because usually when folks asked to talk to the owner, it wasn't just for a pat on the back or a kind word. He asked if we could "talk somewhere private" and right then and there I knew I was in for it! (And I was right.)

With a packed house and little breathing room, I led him away from the hostess stand and down into the package store. It was a brief conversation, and in his typical no-nonsense style, Mr. Neuharth told me who he was, why that mattered and that he'd be spending "a lot of money at the Surf."

In return, he wanted a table ready whenever he came, regardless of the circumstances, no ifs, ands or buts. Mr. Neuharth never wanted himself or any of his important guests to be kept waiting, and expected a table every time, any time, he came into the restaurant.

Without hesitating I said "Yes, sir" and that was the end of the meeting, the end of the discussion and the end of Al's wait for a table from that point forward. As far as I can remember, we always lived up to our promise and had a table waiting for "Mr. Neuharth" whenever he came in, morning, noon or night – even late nights, as you'll soon see.

Like I said, that initial meeting struck the tone for a relationship that I'm proud to say lasted until his death at 89 in his beloved Pumpkin Center. The Surf was far from a sloppy organization. Uncle Bernard had set higher than average standards for himself, and I had tried valiantly to live up to them ever since taking over. Just the same, every restaurant can improve upon quality and, to his credit, Al Neuharth helped us do just that. Not only on his first visit, but for many, many years to come.

He helped me, as a young, new restaurant owner, bring my "A" game every time he walked in the door, and long after he left. And that led to me looking at the restaurant in a new light, and bringing my "A" game any time *any* customer walked through the door, not just a local VIP.

So much of the Surf's success has been a result of good timing. Uncle Bernard had first seen opportunity in Cocoa Beach, when very few others saw it as anything more than just a "sleepy fishing village". Despite a few rocky years after its grand opening in 1948, Bernard's vision proved true and Cocoa Beach became a boom town, thanks mostly to the space program.

Now, in the mid-60s, the Apollo program was in full-bloom and those of us on the Space Coast had grown accustomed to the pomp and circumstance that accompanied any and every space shot.

We often took for granted the presence of astronauts and celebrities that walked in our midst during those launches, but folks like Al Neuharth never let us forget that we were hosting greatness during an unprecedented time in the nation's history. You might say he put things in perspective on a national, even a global level, and for that I am eternally grateful.

Quite frankly, I credit Al with helping make the Surf one of the most popular hangouts for reporters, newscasters, celebrities and, of course, astronauts and engineers during the heyday of the space program, and well beyond.

While the choices for out-of-town movers and shakers were still fairly limited back in the 60s and even the early 70s, Al's stamp of approval gave credibility and credence to the Surf as "the" hangout before, during and after a launch.

I can't even begin to count all the special evenings, events and low-key dinners he hosted for astronauts and their families, foreign dignitaries, rocket scientists – literally – and famous newscasters like David Brinkley and Walter Cronkite and, in later years, their modern counterparts Tom Brokaw, Dan Rather and Peter Jennings.

From intimate gatherings at a table for four or six to catered affairs that required closing off the entire Red Room to accommodate all his VIP guests, Al introduced the Surf to a whole new level of celebrity and, as a result, we became a better organization for it.

Which isn't to say there weren't still a few kinks that needed to be ironed out – at least, according to Mr. Neuharth. Being summoned to Al's home office in his beloved Pumpkin Center was a lot like being sent to the principal's office back when we were still in school: not exactly fun, especially when you're all grown up and think you've got a good handle on your new job title as restaurant owner.

Once Al established residency at the Pumpkin Center we began doing a lot of catering for him. The sprawling oceanfront estate was more office than home back then, and he frequently called his newspaper editors down for lunches or dinners or weekend retreats to bond, talk business and generally brainstorm the company's future.

When Al first asked us if we would be able to cater these and many other special events, we assured him that we could. Of course, the Surf didn't have an official catering business at the time, but we had food, a great wait staff and close proximity to the Pumpkin Center right across the street, so… what could go wrong?

I remember one particularly rushed affair early in our catering agreement with Mr. Neuharth. We were asked to load trays and trays of meats, cheeses and, of course, the Surf's famous steamed jumbo shrimp for one particular party. The only problem was, we didn't have any fancy catering trays the likes of which Al was used to.

Charlie Ragland, my longtime manager, recalls how our salad room diva, Johnny Mae Stephens, suggested that we could use the long sheet pans we used for baking the bread in our bread baskets, cover them with tin foil, garnish them with green, leafy endive and parsley and no one would ever know the difference.

Charlie agreed and Johnny Mae set to work, creating trays we could all be proud of – or so we thought. The party went well, everyone seemed happy and I didn't think twice about it until a few days later when Charlie and I were both "summoned" to a private audience with Mr. Neuharth at the Pumpkin Center.

I can clearly recall the "oh shit" expressions on our faces as Charlie and I heard the news. We both agreed – did we have any other choice?? – and met with Al early the next day. Sitting in his office, we weren't sure what to expect.

Wearing his trademark black and white, Mr. Neuharth got right down to business. He said that he'd been "disappointed" by the party that we catered for him that week and wanted to get a few things straight if we were to keep on catering for him in the future.

"I only have three requests," Charlie recalls Mr. Neuharth saying that fateful day as we both leaned forward, like kids in the principal's office, prepared to get a lesson – and did we ever! "First, I don't like peanuts in my mixed nuts."

Charlie and I sat back in our seats, exhaling loudly. "Done," I recall Charlie exclaiming as I nodded in agreement, still waiting for the other two shoes to drop.

"Second, I expect every tray you serve at my parties to look the same at the end of the night as it does at the beginning of the night. Do you understand?"

Charlie and I looked at each other, nodding carefully. We both knew exactly what he wanted, and it would prove to be one of the most challenging aspects of catering one of Al's parties, or any party for that matter.

What Mr. Neuharth meant was that if we had a platter of steamed shrimp sitting on a table, it had better look as full, as plentiful, as appetizing, as appealing and as *overflowing* at midnight as it did during cocktail hour five or six hours earlier when the party was just beginning.

You know how at most parties, by the end of the night, the platters look a lot worse for the wear? Half the crackers are gone, the garnish is wilting, the crackers are a little stale and the shrimp are all gone? Not for Mr. Neuharth.

Charlie was my operations guy. If something had to get from Point A to Point B, and look darn good when it arrived, he'd make it happen no matter how far the distance or how plentiful the obstacles. He later told me that for the rest of the meeting that morning, his mind was spinning with how to fill Al's request.

What it meant, he said, was that if Mr. Neuharth wanted 400 pounds of shrimp for a party, Charlie would have to prepare at least 800… so that there would always be a heaping platter waiting for guests, whether they arrived promptly when the party started or at the last minute.

We nodded, waiting for Mr. Neuharth's third request. Finally, with a wry smile, he delivered. "Also," he said, sitting back in his chair as if enjoying our mounting anxiety. "I'm pretty sure there are restaurant supply stores that sell silver platters for outfits like yourself. Why don't you guys look into that before my *next* party?"

And with that, the meeting was over, and Charlie and I had just gotten our first lesson in Catering 101. Trust me, it wasn't to be our last, but I have to say we wound up a better outfit for it.

Playing Favorites: *Juli and Maria*

We quickly learned that, in addition to his Three Unbroken Rules for Catering (as Charlie and I referred to them ever after), Mr. Neuharth also had his "favorites" when it came to certain Surf employees. When he came in to eat at the restaurant, nothing would do but to have Juli Shroble wait on him, often hand and foot.

Through trial and error and tons of patience, Juli learned just what the man wanted, oftentimes in advance of his even ordering. Juli fondly – or occasionally "not" so fondly – recalls many evenings when Al would come in just before closing time, saunter back to the Red Room with a few of his editors and have a late night "meeting," fully catered by Juli and whoever was unlucky enough to be working the kitchen and bar that night.

His late-night meetings meant that Juli and several other select crew members had a late night as well, because we had to keep a bartender and at least one cook on duty so that they could provide whatever it was – and I do mean "whatever" it was – that Mr. Neuharth wanted for he and his guests.

When it came to catering Mr. Neuharth's many and well-attended events, we were fortunate to find Maria Meagher, who started as a waitress at the Surf but soon rose to prominence in our brand new catering division.

Mr. Neuharth loved Maria, and if you've ever been to one of his parties, or pretty much any party catered by the Surf in the last thirty years or so, you're likely to have met, and fallen in love with, Maria as well.

She's a go getter with a capital "G" and it was no surprise Neuharth insisted that Maria cater every one of his parties. And I do mean everyone. If it was a small, intimate affair, Maria might be there grilling steaks at the Pumpkin Center. If it was 150 guests milling about the back lawn rubbing shoulders with Tom Brokaw or a shuttle commander, Maria was right there, her trademark laugh echoing throughout the property as she poured champagne or swung by with a tray of appetizers.

I'll give Neuharth this much: he had great taste in women! Both Juli and Maria would have to be high on my list of all-time, Top-10 greatest Surf employees, and I'm glad to count them both as friends – even family –as well. I'd like to think that, between barking orders and making demands, Al Neuharth felt the same way. (And I'm pretty sure he did.)

Price Check!

I can vividly recall one night when we had changed the prices on our wine list, a rare ordeal that necessitated printing new wine menus and alerting our most regular customers to the price hike of their favorite wines as well. Apparently, Mr. Neuharth got an old menu one night and, after ordering several bottles of his favorite Pouilly-Fousse, was handed a check listing the new price.

The newspaper man was famous for his attention to detail and, of course, he spotted the price discrepancy right away. Despite the fact that his bill couldn't have amounted to more than five or ten dollars over the usual amount, he felt he'd been "cheated" and wouldn't let the event go unrecognized – or uncorrected.

Shortly afterward, Charlie and I were both summoned back to Pumpkin Center for another meeting with the man himself. This time, instead of speaking directly to us, Mr. Neuharth addressed his two dogs, one black, one white. While Charlie and I worked diligently to hide our surprise, Al consulted the dogs as he proceeded with his quite unusual Q & A.

"So," he might ask the white dog, "what do you think I should do with these boys?"

Or, he might say to the black one, "Do you think they've learned their lesson yet?"

Charlie and I kept waiting for him to address us, personally, but for the entire meeting it was just Mr. Neuharth and his dogs. Afterward, walking back across the street to the Surf, I turned to Charlie and said, "I can't tell you how close I was to just getting up and walking out of that meeting."

Charlie agreed, but added, "That would have been pretty stupid of us, huh?"

If we weren't being summoned to Pumpkin Center for one misdeed or another, Charlie or I would occasionally receive one of Mr. Neuharth's "lessons" on his personalized – and very recognizable – stationary.

Trust me, you couldn't miss it! It was the same color as the banner of Florida Today, a kind of reddish-orange, and had matching envelopes and stationery. Again, these were never greeting cards, condolences or get-well notes, but rather they were "teaching opportunities" on everything from the perfect temperature of a medium rare steak to how to pour a bottle of red wine without dripping on the tablecloth to the lighting over his favorite booth in the Red Room.

I later learned that Charlie and I weren't the only ones to receive Al's legendary "teaching" note cards. In fact, when I attended his funeral shortly after his death, it was clear that the man was legendary for sending them to his entire staff as well.

I suppose, in a way, I should find that comforting, perhaps even flattering. After all, some very, very talented people worked for Al Neuharth, and if *they* screwed up and got letters from time to time, I guess Charlie and I weren't so bad after all.

But trust me, it never felt like a compliment at the time!

The Last Supper

One final story says a lot about Al Neuharth's own personal sense of style, craftsmanship and humor. While the paper he founded, *USA Today*, might be considered one of the widest read newspapers in the country today, there were apparently some rocky times during its first few years.

One party the Surf catered during those uncertain early days of *USA Today* has since come to be known as "The Last Supper." That's how Al referred to it as we planned the event and, after attending it, I'm sure that's how his honored "guests" felt about it as well.

I remember the event vividly, probably because it was one of the few Al ever asked me to personally oversee. It was a Sunday afternoon, 4 o' clock on the dot, and Al had summoned the original team that had put *USA Today* together to the Surf.

When they walked into the private dining room just off the bar area reserved exclusively for Al's "Last Supper," they saw their paper's founder sitting in a chair behind a table loaded with traditional Jewish foods, wearing a monk-like robe and… a crown of thorns.

As they sat around, nervously waiting for what might come next, they didn't have to wait long: Mr. Neuharth expressed his disappointment with their performance thus far and blamed them for making him take such drastic measures to get their attention on the need to cut operating costs.

Al then launched into a series of apostolic-sounding quotes with each beginning "thou shalt…", which brought assorted reactions from those assembled. Some were puzzled, some just smiled. Board Chairman Paul Mill alternated between scowling and smiling and editor John Quinn, a former altar boy, walked out of the meeting altogether!

Of course, Al was not without his own "unique" sense of humor. Shortly after his diatribe, he had the meager meal removed from the table in front of him and in came much more festive platters loaded down with shrimp, steamed lobster, steaks, seafood and more. Still, as usual, Al got his message across. Shape up, or else. And to their credit, his team went back to work determined to please their boss.

The meeting, and the man, got results.

All of which is not to say that Al Neuharth was not a generous benefactor or willing mentor, if only by leading through example. While spare with his words, his actions spoke volumes about, I feel, his fondness for myself or, at least, the Surf. Year after year, in good times and in bad, the Surf and I were a part of Al's life and, I like to think, vice versa.

He was a generous man, in his way. I'll never forget the time Al overheard me talking about having to go to Manhattan to attend a hospital bond closing and trying to figure out the best place to stay.

He generously offered us the use of his apartment in the city and, as if that weren't enough, when we arrived at his spacious penthouse, even found a chilled bottle of champagne in the fridge!

In later years I can recall he invited my wife and I to be guests of his at an informal reunion of the original Mercury/Apollo astronauts. Not to serve him or wait on him, but to sit alongside Al, his wife and several heroes of mine, legends like Al Shepard, John Glenn, Deke Slayton and Wally Schirra.

Although we occasionally clashed and he could be a challenging task master, as I'm sure his employees at Gannett, *Florida Today* and later *USA Today* would agree, I believe they'd also agree their boss – and on many occasions, mine – was a generous and giving mentor who led by example, and always in a forward direction.

In later years, Al had time to write several books, including one titled *Confessions of an SOB*, with the subtitle: "A Maverick CEO Reveals How You Can… Outfox Your Enemies, Outcharm Your Friends, Outdo Yourself… and Have a Lot of Fun!"

Al called his key colleagues together to give each one a copy, whereupon his longtime editor and colleague John Quinn announced that he was writing a book of the rest of the Neuharth story, titled, "Confessions of a BOS, as in Big Old Softie," with the other side of the story!

In fact, at Mr. Neuharth's funeral in 2013, I heard firsthand how many Gannett employees felt about their boss, and I felt honored to be in a room with so many others honoring the great man we had all lost far too soon.

For not only did Al Neuharth help, in his own way, put Bernard's Surf on the map but he also helped forge a young new restaurateur's passion for excellence in his own organization, however humble compared to the nation's most read newspaper.

Chapter 7:

Rocket Years

Idon't think I'd be overstating things to say that without a space program, there would have been no Bernard's Surf. Indeed, I believe most residents and local businessmen who watched the Space Coast grow beyond our wildest dreams in the 60s, 70s and 80s and even still today would readily agree with me.

The Surf began way back in 1948 with my Uncle Bernard's stubborn insistence that Cocoa Beach and, indeed, all of Brevard would grow along with the building of Patrick Air Force Base, to the south, and Canaveral Air Force Station, to the north. Located centrally between both government installations, Bernard's forethought proved to be both timely *and* correct.

Having been here from the very beginning of the space program, I can tell you that I can't remember a time when there wasn't some type of activity going on at the space center, in all its incarnations, from Cape Kennedy to Kennedy Space Center to present day, with new outfits like SpaceX and Blue Horizons entering the fray.

From groundbreakings to visiting dignitaries to actual launches, my family and I have grown up in the shadow of the Space Coast and have been fortunate enough to work alongside so many principal players in the founding of our country's space program.

It's been amazing to watch launches go off on Thursday knowing that you fed the very astronauts sitting in the capsule on Tuesday! It's incredible watching the visible reaction of an entire restaurant full of people when a hero like John Glenn or Alan Shepard walks through the doors, and even more so when they walk straight over and greet you by name! Trust me, the wave of admiration and pure awe as it crosses each customer's face, from one to the next, is truly something to behold.

Having watched so many launches in my career, often by merely walking out the front door of the Surf and shielding my eyes against the Florida sun and glancing up into the brilliant blue sky over Cocoa Beach, it's easy to take such heroes for granted.

But looking back on it now, I can tell you that the whole area got excited before, during and after a launch. Every launch. These were the true days of the "space race," that frenzied period in the 1960s when we were trying to beat Russia into space and, later, working under President Kennedy's mandate to put a man on the moon by the end of the decade.

Everything was new and untested. From the rocket fuel used to propel those giant missiles into space to the circumference of the launch pads to the surface of the rockets to the rockets themselves. It was all cutting edge even if now, looking back, those very rockets can seem outdated and even ancient by our modern, high-tech standards.

If you've ever met a pilot, you know the kind of mettle and confidence it takes to fly a jet filled with fuel across the sky. Take that confidence and apply it twenty-fold when talking about an astronaut, whose job it is to sit atop an immense rocket filled with highly flammable fuel and blast off into the unknown, hundreds of miles above the planet.

After awhile you could spot an astronaut without even knowing his name. And, of course, back then they were all men. Bearing the traditional flat top of a fighter pilot and the physical bearing of a prize fighter, these brave men looked daring even when jammed into a suit for one of the press conferences they always looked so uncomfortable attending.

Of course, over drinks and dinner in the Red Room, they usually relaxed and were more than happy to tell stories about the space program and what it felt like to sit atop a lighted rocket. When you could fight your way through the bevy of beauties asking them for their autographs, that is.

See a Launch, Get a Free Drink

When I took over the Surf in the mid-60s, I inherited more than just a restaurant, but a legacy that was directly linked to the space coast, in general, and the space program, in particular. Launches had been going on for years, and with each one Bernard the entrepreneur had found a way to capitalize on the booming space program and the accompanying space coast.

Hotels weren't the only businesses in town to turn rocket names into surefire rocket fuel for their cash registers. For its part, the Surf featured a variety of space-themed drinks to entice tourists to be a part of the space program, if only by hoisting a glass and launching themselves into a nice, safe buzz!

There was the "Moon Shot," for instance, made with 151-proof rum, vodka and cream for just $1.50. Or if you preferred you could order an "Apollo" made from Galliano, vodka and lime juice on the rocks for just $1.75. If you were in the mood for fast and quick, you could order a "Thor," which featured a no frills – if high-octane – combination of vodka, gin and scotch… for just a dollar!

Or if you had a larger group there was always the crowd pleasing – not to mention downright confusing – "Astro-son," featuring Irish gin, a "whisper of vermouth" (I'm quoting directly from the menu here) and a Bermuda onion (!!), all set aflame because… why not? It would set you back six whole bucks but would serve four or five, depending on which of you ate the onion!

Or, if you'd had your fill of the space program after buying souvenir T-shirts up and down A1A all day and wanted something simple, cheap and cold, you could still grab a small Michelob draft for twenty cents or a full yard of Lowenbrau for only $1.50. Whatever your speed or taste, the Surf offered drinks for just about every shot, astronaut and planet in the solar system.

While I'd like to give Bernard sole credit for these creative cocktail mixes, having stood behind a bar for close to 50 years I can tell you that a more likely scenario is that after a few of their own cocktails, several jovial and well-meaning bar patrons would get creative and want Bernard to fix them a "Saturn" or a "Moon Shot."

"What's in that?" I could picture Bernard asking with a wink, a clean bar towel tossed over his shoulder just in case someone should leave a drink ring on the bar.

"Let's find out," I can picture the bar crowd laughing as they created yet another drink for the ever-expanding cocktail menu, watching as Bernard mixed a little scotch, a little rum, a little juice and a garnish – or even tossing in an onion – to create the next "drink special" of the month.

Eventually the list of cosmic cocktails grew to the point where they were blown up to poster size and featured behind the bar, no longer small enough to grace the pages of a simple cocktail menu. One such poster sits, framed, in my son Rhett's house. (Although I had to borrow it off the wall for a few weeks to help me write this chapter.)

During family gatherings we fondly read out the names and always the prices, imagining a simpler, kinder and definitely cheaper era where for less than two bucks you could get slightly tipsy on a drink named after your favorite astronaut, solar system or spaceship!

Of course, a full bar and some funny-sounding drinks weren't all I inherited from Uncle Bernard. If you were lucky enough to be sitting at the bar during a launch, your drink was on the house; every time. The tradition started with the earliest launches from Cape Canaveral during the late 50s and early 60s, and lasted all through the heady days of the space shuttle program in the 80s and 90s.

A plaque over the Surf bar featured the legend, "Anyone at the bar during a missile launch shall recieve a free drink." No, that's not a typo. The original plaque maker must have never heard the old "I before E except after C" rule and carved it that way instead. Since we never had it redone – it was, after all, a piece of history as far as we were concerned – for years every time a launch went up some smart aleck would remind me that the sign was misspelled.

We gave him a free drink anyway!

Rockets Weren't the Only Things Booming...

You could feel the energy all over town when the space center was prepping for a launch. Traffic would slow down to a crawl as reporters and tourists alike came flooding into town, turning A1A into a parking lot on your way to or from work.

Business would pick up all over town, not just in the Surf but at Ramon's and George's Steakhouse, the Mousetrap and Wolfie's as well. The hotels would be full, and guests had their choice from a sea of mostly one and two story 60s era hotels, all of which naturally featured rocket-themed names to match the Space Coast aesthetic.

If I recall correctly, there was the Satellite Motel, which featured a giant globe on its sign, the Astrocraft and the Starlite Motels, both of which featured a rocket on their sign design, and of course the Polaris and the Atlantis.

Long before Cocoa Beach and Central Florida became tourist destinations, it was already a Mecca for space enthusiasts and the day-to-day workers related to the space program.

It wasn't just astronauts who needed rooms at the Holiday Inn and the Ramada, the Sea Missile or the Silver Sands, but the reporters, the photographers, the radio announcers and the TV newscasters, all looking for a nice, cold drink at the end of another long day of filing stories, snapping pictures or filling in the editors back in the home office.

One by one they'd file into the Surf, hungry or thirsty and eager to get indoors after another day spent baking in the Florida heat. Most were northerners, lead men from the big papers in New York or Chicago or DC, unaccustomed to the full brunt of Cocoa Beach's natural – and year-round – sunshine. No wonder Bernard had been so eager to put the words "air-conditioned lounge" right on the cover of his earliest menus!

As the night wore on and tongues would loosen, you'd get your fill of space program gossip. Which rocket jockey was the biggest carouser, the most energetic womanizer, who could drink the most, or stay out the latest and still get up for a five-mile run on the beach the next morning.

It was a playground for most, a mini vacation for others and the astronauts themselves were often the most vocal supporters of this fraternity atmosphere.

We all have our favorite astronaut stories, and if you grew up on or even near the Space Coast you likely have your own favorites as well. Even if you were just a visitor, lucky enough to have dinner alongside one of the original Mercury or Apollo astronauts, you've got a story or two to tell.

In this chapter, I'll share a few of my own:

Table for One

What amazes me is how many movers and shakers drifted through the crowd at the Surf in those heady years, unnoticed as they sat down, had a cocktail or two, enjoyed their relish tray and breadbasket, ate their meal, paid and then left.

The whole while, their closest neighbors were none the wiser that they'd just sat next to, say, a big-time reporter for the *New York Times* or my old friend Jack King, who for decades was "the voice of NASA," counting down just about every launch you ever heard with his smooth, velvety style.

Other times, you were often in such awe of some of these people that you never knew what to say or how to react when they walked in. One busy night I remember a distinguished looking gentleman coming in and asking Norma, the hostess that night, for a table for one.

There was this one little table for two in the corner, with a chair that had been borrowed for a bigger party, I suppose, that was now quite literally a table for one. Norma led the man to it and I watched as Wernher von Braun, the father of rocket technology and legendary mastermind behind the Saturn V rocket booster that helped land the first men on the moon, sat down to study the Surf menu.

It was such an odd sight to watch the whole room gradually, inexplicably shift their attention toward this great man, then back again toward their companions, murmuring about his fabled accomplishments and marveling at their proximity to greatness. As the evening wore on people would quietly, respectfully approach and introduce themselves or shake his hand or ask for an autograph, and then slowly return to their seat.

And as he left it struck me that here was this great man, this powerhouse of the space age, sitting in a crowded restaurant eating dinner and no one had bothered to ask him to sit with them. Few of them probably remember the lone diner in his stiff suit and stiffer accent, but I do, and I'll never forget it.

Unfortunately, not all my memories are pleasant ones:

NASA's First Disaster

According to Space.com, "On Jan. 27, 1967, NASA experienced its first space disaster – the deaths of three astronauts during a training exercise for the Apollo 1 mission... Edward H. White II, Virgil I. 'Gus' Grissom, and Roger B. Chaffee. A fire inside the Apollo Command Module during a test took the lives of all three astronauts."

Well, that's the official version, anyway. I was there that night, working at the Surf, washing glasses and pouring drinks behind the bar as usual. In attendance were a smattering of national press and hardnosed reporters, waiting on results of the test that would ultimately take the doomed crew's life.

Someone called the bar that night, I can't remember who it was now, so many years later, to let me know what had happened. But they told me what they knew and I turned to the lounge full of reporters. Not wanting to cause a panic, I went around the room, approaching each journalist one at a time to tell them as much as I knew.

In minutes, it seemed, the lounge was deserted and soon the news of the disastrous fire that took the lives of three brave astronauts – Edward H. White II, Virgil I. "Gus" Grissom, and Roger B. Chaffee – would spread all over the world.

We all knew the potential for disaster, of course. That's why NASA ran such tests: to face the worst-case scenario and make sure it never happened in real life. But this was the first time we realized just *how* courageous these brave men and women were, and how high the cost could be when something finally went wrong.

Comrades in Arms; Menus in... Russian?!?

After years of watching the US space program try to outwit, outman and outdistance the Russians in the "race for space," it was a welcome relief in the mid-1970s when both sides of the "space race" came together for something called the Apollo-Soyuz Test Project.

The mission was designed to bring both Russian astronauts – or cosmonauts, as they were known in their homeland – and American astronauts together in space. Picture a temporary space station, designed for just one mission, and you'll get a feel for what both countries were trying to achieve with this historic project.

Featuring joint launches and a special space attachment that would unite both countries via a unique docking mechanism, the Apollo-Soyuz mission capped off nearly two decades of intense competition between both countries, and proved an exciting adventure for those of us on earth watching it all play out on the evening news each night.

It happened in the summer of 1975, with joint launches from both countries – in less than eight hours of each other – on July 15th. The two ships docked in space two days later, on the 17th of July, to celebrations on both ends. The docking mechanism was successful and the captains of each mission shook hands mid-flight, even assembling a joint plaque to commemorate the mission.

Then Soviet premier Leonid Brezhnev wrote a statement for the cosmonauts to read, and the astronauts received a call from US President Gerald Ford. After nearly two days linked together the two ships parted ways, with the Apollo crew returning to earth several days later.

But before the mission ever got off the ground, the Surf made a little history of its own. Months before the July mission was actually set to commence, on February 8, 1975, we were honored to be able to host the American astronauts and Russian cosmonauts who would be going on the mission with a commemorative meal at the Surf. To say I was nervous was the understatement of the year, but looking back I can honestly say I was proud to be a part of such a historic event.

To make the Cosmonauts feel welcome, we had a special dinner featuring many local and/or Florida delicacies including Canaveral shrimp, Indian River crab claws, stone crabs from the Florida Keys plus Florida lobster tail. There was crab bisque, fried shrimp ala Ruth and fried snapper ala Doris and, of course, Florida key lime pie for dessert. I had even printed out special menus for the occasion, in both English and Russian, as souvenirs the VIP guests could take home. It was kind of a big deal, being reported on in both our local and national papers as a celebration of the historic mission that captivated two nations.

One of the personal highlights for me was when Soyuz mission commander Alexei Leonov drew his version of the linked space vessels, mid-flight, while autographing one of the regular Surf menus! To this day, it's one of my most treasured possessions and sits front and center in the front entranceway at Rusty's at the Port.

Most of the night was a blur of excited anticipation and tense nerves. It's one thing to be deep in space or cloistered at NASA, but for such international figures to dine together in a public place, a busy restaurant no less, is apparently a bit of a security nightmare. So hours before the event we had security from both countries doggedly checking all the nooks and crannies of the Surf, scrutinizing employees – and even myself – for possible security breaches!

An article written about the event for *Today* newspaper – I told you it was kind of a big deal! – alludes to the security issues faced that night with a humorous story that happened on the way into the restaurant. The cosmonauts were transported by bus from a cocktail party earlier that evening at the Holiday Inn just up the road. When these highly-trained astronauts arrived in the Surf parking lot they were approached by "two long-haired youths asking what 'convention' they were from"! Tongues firmly planted in cheeks, the security agents explained they were "a group of shoe salesmen" and quickly sent the two hippies on their way.

Security concerns aside, I can honestly say the night went off (mostly) without a hitch. Why do I say mostly? Well, I can admit now that I was the one who decided to serve French wine that night!

Along for the Ride

The devastating low of the Apollo Command Module fire that cost the lives of three brave astronauts – Ed White, Gus Grissom and Roger B. Chaffee – stood in sharp contrast to the highs of the Apollo-Soyuz Test Project. And yet both momentous events reflect the tenuous nature of a program that, let's not forget, is designed to launch human beings into space on giant, fuel-propelled rockets.

And so while we like to remember the highlights of the space program, as well as the many joys of life on the Space Coast, as someone who's been along for the ride during the entire space program, I can tell you that it hasn't always been easy, for the astronauts, the crews, the community or the local merchants who serve them all, and in many ways depend on them for their livelihoods.

Between the ticker tape parades and successful launches, between the new launch pads and seasoned reporters crowding our bars before, during and after a launch, Cocoa Beach grew both alongside of – and in the shadows of – the American space program.

While many will think the space center is all we built a city around, the fact is we've always had to make do with the fits and starts of a federally funded program that has had its own trials and errors, celebrations and setbacks.

Between the Apollo missions and the space shuttle, there were entire years, many of them in fact, where not much was happening at

Cape Kennedy and, later, Kennedy Space Center. In the meantime, we had to make do.

And that's just what we did. You could see the changes in the town over the years. While we never lost our admiration of, respect for or fascination with the space program, little by little it quit being such a dominant force in the local landscape.

One by one the hotels that had once been named after rockets and space programs were bought up by the national chains, or simply changed their names to reflect the modern reality of an evolving "space" coast.

Between launches and parades, and the occasional years-long dry spells between them, it was the beach that drew tourists, year after year, in good times and in bad. And so the hotels changed their names from Atlantis and Polaris to more tourist-friendly titles, with "sand" and "sea" on their signs instead of "moon" and "rocket".

People move on and forget. Even looking at the drink menu Bernard and his regular bar patrons created over the years, celebrating capsules and missions and rockets gone by, most people wouldn't even recognize the names of most of the missiles, or the missions, these days.

Thor? Mace? The Centaur? The Juno II? The Enos? Who remembers those names anymore? Hell, I must have glanced at that drink menu hundreds of times over the years and even I don't remember them.

So while I have fond memories of those bustling launch days and parades and fondly cherish the many brave men and women I've met who had a hand in the space program, not just the astronauts who took the glory but the engineers and techs and scientists who made their missions possible, I remember too the hard times that made running a restaurant for over 50 years more than just an accomplishment, but a near impossibility.

I can smile about it now but many were the sleepless nights when the Surf was on the chopping block. National recessions led to local recessions, and every new decade, it seemed, brought some new struggle, challenge or obstacle to overcome. In addition to financial struggles, there were the inevitable personal and professional struggles to overcome as well.

Chapter 8:

Continuing a Tradition... While Making it My Own

As the 60s gradually faded away and the 70s wore on, I finally began to get the hang of this restaurant business. They were busy times, with rocket launches coming more and more frequently and, with them, boat loads of tourists to watch the launches.

Thanks to its early reputation as one of the first, and best, restaurant-slash-cocktail lounges on the beach, the Surf had a strong brand and a lasting tradition. Now, as I began to grow more and more confident in my skills as a new business owner and leader, I sought to make the Surf my own.

My days usually started early, in my office, pouring over the latest liquor order for the bar. After that I would wander over from my office and make the rounds in the restaurant itself. And that's when I got to see all the talented people who made the Surf so special all those years:

Bo Pete, a Living Legend

I'd always stop in and chat with Bo Pete Kirkland, our long-time meat cutter-slash-chauffer, who had usually just arrived in his trademark white van bearing most of the kitchen staff from his morning rounds.

Pete would arrive promptly every morning at nine, with the day's kitchen crew pouring out of the long white van and getting straight to work. In the afternoons between 2 and 3, Pete would drive the day shift home, grab a change of clothes and then pick up the night shift, arriving back at the Surf between 4 and 5 with another van load of employees. Later, after a long night shift, around 11:30 or so, Pete would drive the last of the day's kitchen staff home, only to start the process all over again bright and early the next morning.

Pete's brother, Leroy Kirkland, worked for many years as a cook in our kitchen, and was even featured on our menu for his famous Leroy's fried chicken.

Every Wednesday for years I would sit with my brother Ronnie and our father, Lou, to discuss business, family, plans for the future, the economy, the city and the county. In addition to the usual cocktails, Leroy's fried chicken was often the highlight of the meal.

Over the years, Pete became less like an employee and more like a family member. He was also a jack of all trades, equal parts chauffer, Human Resources manager, meat cutter, bartender and caterer extraordinaire. Many of you reading this will know Bo Pete by his face, by his laugh, by his boisterous spirit, if not by his name.

He's bartended my weddings, even my kid's weddings, but often only in spirit. After pouring a few drinks he'd quickly pass on the duties to whoever he'd brought along to help him and then come on out and mingle, one of the party... one of the family.

While many restaurants have a high turnover (and that can certainly be said of the Surf at certain times during its history), for years Pete drove the same loyal employees back and forth in his trusty white van.

Yes, the van itself needed to be replaced every few years, and who wouldn't after all the miles Pete put on it driving folks back and forth, twice a day, seven days a week? And, yes, new faces came and went.

Such is the nature of the restaurant business, after all. It's hard work, and lots of it, night after night, day after day. Busy shifts and slow shifts, slicing and dicing, preparing and frying, hot ovens and steaming dishwashers and complaining patrons and everyone wanting something, all the time, often all at once.

But through all of this, year after year, Pete and his brother Leroy Kirkland got on and off the van, as did other folks who never seemed to age, although that was probably just us seeing each other so often throughout the days. (They probably all watched me age plenty over the years!)

Few folks ever peer beyond the swinging kitchen doors to take a good look at what makes a restaurant tick, but let me invite you on a guided tour:

You might have known your favorite waitress, or even hostess, and especially bartender if you came into the Surf over the years.

Depending on how old, or young, you were when you got your first taste of our famous onion board, relish tray or fried mullet.

But the folks in the kitchen made the rest of our jobs possible. You can't serve fine food if you don't have clean plates, and so you've got to have a crack dishwasher – and, on some shifts, even two or three – to make sure those plates are clean and stacked and stocked and cleaned and stacked and stocked some more.

You can't have a great half-and-half salad on a hot summer day without the folks in the salad room slicing the fresh avocados and picking shells out of the fresh crabmeat and steaming and peeling the shrimp ahead of time. We never bought pre-packaged food in those days, so every fried shrimp had to be made by hand.

That means cleaning them, deveining them, peeling them, then dipping them in milk, cracker crumbs, more milk, corn meal, more milk and a final dusting of flour.

Same for our homemade onion rings and so on. All of that takes time, patience and lots of man hours, and that's what our kitchen staff brought to the table – brought to *your* table – every day, all year, for the 50-plus years the Surf was in business.

And there I'd be, making my rounds, day in and day out, trying to keep it all together. As I made my way through the restaurant each day, Pete would be slicing beef throughout the morning and well into the afternoon, before he'd drive the day shift home and pick up most of the night shift, a duty he performed until the Surf closed many, many years later.

"Where Everybody Knows Your Name"

After checking on the kitchen each morning I'd make it onto the house floor, greeting the servers on shift that day and the few early birds already seated at the bar. I'd be there, too, helping whoever was bartending by washing glasses and pouring drinks or opening bottles or tapping draft beers, whatever the lunch rush required.

I always felt comfortable behind the bar, maybe because I knew where everything was and, what's more, *who* everyone was. The regulars came and went, keeping up a running dialogue that lasted, for many of them, for years.

Year in, year out, I heard about their good news and bad news, their wives, siblings, children and, later, grandchildren. The Surf was a home away from home for lots of folks, at least during lunch and dinner, and regulars were a lot like family.

Eventually I'd make it out from behind the bar and do my rounds, walking around the floor, pressing the flesh, meeting new people and greeting regulars, often at the very same table.

After lunch, there were more small fires to put out, decisions to make and paperwork to do in my office. I'd eat a small meal, usually at the bar, before heading home for a quick nap before I'd shower and get into another three-piece suit for the night shift.

Dinner was often a repeat of lunch: paperwork, rows of figures, brush fires to put out, folks to meet and greet, ice to pour, glasses to wash, cold beer on tap and more jokes and stories with the folks at the bar.

After the dinner rush was over and the restaurant was closed for the night, around 10 or 11 if we were lucky, it was time for the rest of us to grab a quick meal, a drink or two and unwind. Unwinding might take a few hours, and by the time the place had cleared out for the night, with both employees and guests heading home, it might be midnight or later. Sometimes, a *lot* later.

And that was before we opened Across the Street... across the street!

Chapter 9:

Across the Street... And Over the Edge!

To give you some sense of the geography that existed around 2 South Atlantic Avenue back in the late 1970s, at least according to my best recollection, Moe's Missile Lounge used to be directly east of Bernard's Surf, in that little shopping center between Coconuts and the Surf, where the shell shop is directly across from Nature's Habit today.

Owned by Moe Kirschenbaum, Malcolm and Jack's father, the Missile Lounge took up the entire front half of the building at the intersection of Minutemen Causeway and A1A, from the shell shop to the Italian restaurant that is there today. Back then, there was a little package store there and, how should I put this delicately... an adult lounge... for lack of a better term.

When Real-Life Monopoly Gets Ugly

Now, directly across the street from the Surf, to the North, was a little dress shop called Marcene Mode's. It sat on the property where Yen-Yen's is to this day. Unfortunately, Marcene Mode's was going out of business and they were looking to sell the building, the property and the parking lot behind it.

Being good neighbors, and perhaps figuring our pockets were a little deeper than they actually were, the owner came to us and asked if we wanted to buy it. Dad still owned the Surf at the time, and he wasn't interested in stretching the Fischer Seafood business into another new property.

But Moe Kirschenbaum was, and he agreed to buy the building instead. He opened up a store called, "Ye Old Court Shop." Not only that, but he decided to bring his infamous girly bar along for the ride, and installed it in the building to the back of the old Marcene Mode's.

Well, Dad was incensed. Though far from a prude, he was a businessman and a family businessman to boot, and he felt the current zoning was all wrong for "that kind of club" in a family resort area. So he fought the move tooth and nail.

I was there, stuck in the middle, as usual during those days. The Surf was mine, in look and feel and management and general operations, but it was still Dad's on paper and so I had to kind of toe the line – or else – in those days.

Moe's son, Malcolm, was and still is a good friend of mine, as well as my longtime attorney. During this turbulent time, he often stopped in with our mutual friend Frank Wolf – of Wolfie's Lounge fame – to try and talk me through what was happening and possibly soothe old family wounds.

In retrospect it sounds petty, I suppose, but you can never argue with the goings on in a small beach town, be it business or personal. Feathers get ruffled, everybody knows everybody's business, and it can become hard to navigate at times.

Things got pretty heated at one point, between the politics and the zoning and the "us versus them" moments between me and my Dad and me and my friends, and I'll never forget standing out in A1A after closing the Surf one night, hashing things out with Frank Wolf in the middle of the deserted street at one in the morning!

At some point, Moe Kirschenbaum passed away, and the fate of his Missile Lounge and the adjoining nightclub hung in limbo. I don't know if Dad had any regrets about how his last few meetings with Moe had gone but, if he did, he never shared them with me.

The Surf was busy, I had work to do and I assumed the issue of the building "across the street" would all work out in the end. Well, it did and it didn't!

A Fateful Meeting

One night not long after Moe's passing, his wife, Terry, and their son, Malcolm, came into the Surf and asked me to have dinner with them. I figured it was as good a time as any to break bread and make peace, so I willingly obliged.

After some pleasant conversation and a cocktail or two, the

discussion soon turned to business. Malcolm finally said, "Listen, Rusty, we want to sell this place, and we want $125,000 for it."I nodded and told them I'd need to think about it, though in my head I was secretly thinking, "Okay, this could be good." Part of my reasoning was because one of the stipulations of the deal was that the property came with the pretty sizable parking lot area just north of where Yen Yen's is today. I thought, even if the building and any business we opened there might be a wash, that property was valuable enough in and of itself as Cocoa Beach continued to grow and expand, particularly around the downtown area.

The only hiccup was that I had to agree to keep one of the lots attached to the building if I were ever to sell, which seemed insignificant at the time but would come back to haunt me many, many years later.

And so, the building directly "across the street" from the Surf was soon officially ours. We owned it, lock, stock and barrel, and now the only question was: what the hell were we going to do with it?

Location, Location, Location

I hadn't really paid much attention to what we were actually buying or even why – until it was officially ours. Then panic set in, and Charlie and I walked over to check it out officially. Well, it was a lot of different things at the time, and none of anything special.

The building itself had housed all kinds of different businesses in the past, from a casino to a dress shop to a liquor store, a nightclub, complete with worn brass rails and leather furniture. It was dark and dingy and smoky and I don't recall there being a single window, despite sitting across the street from the beautiful and scenic Atlantic Ocean.

Still, it had potential. Tons of room under a single roof, plenty of parking, and a prime location right there at the intersection of Minuteman Causeway and A1A. You couldn't get any more "Main Street" Cocoa Beach if you wanted to; and now it was all ours.

It was a big space, that much was true, but it would need a lot of work to bring up to The Surf standards, which Bernard had set fairly high and I had tried to keep high ever since taking over in the 60s.

Still, Charlie and I both thought it was a great opportunity to tap into Cocoa Beach's booming nightlife scene without the burden of serving a full menu. And for me, that was a relief indeed.

Not that bars were easy to run by any means, but compared to a full kitchen staff, food and production costs, spoilage, shrinkage and everything else that goes along with a complete and thorough dinner menu the likes of which we featured at the Surf, opening a pure "lounge only" seemed like a walk around the park versus a Boston marathon! Other than the startup and liquor costs, the business would have a low overhead and high potential for profits.

At least, that's how I sold it to the loan officers at the bank and my father, Lou, who together pitched in to make the building across the street from the Surf a reality. And what a reality it was! Although I'd been behind the bar for years, washing glasses and pouring regulars draft beer straight from the tap, I'd never run an actual lounge, or started one up from scratch.

After all, I'd come to the Surf in a turnkey fashion. In other words, the business itself was already up and running when I walked in. I didn't have to pour over blueprints or ensure the kitchen was up to code, pull permits or haggle over where this table would go or what our maximum occupancy was at any given time. I just had to assume ownership, turn my key in the door, step in for my uncle and get to work.

This new venture was another animal altogether, and one I can now readily admit I wasn't necessarily prepared for at the time. That didn't stop me, though. As usual, I rolled up my sleeves and got to work, brother in arms – and now partner in crime – general manager Charlie Ragland right by my side.

Since we had no idea what to do with it, but definitely wanted to make our money back, Charlie and I set off on what we called a "fact finding mission" to get the best bang for our buck.

We wanted to see what was out there on the entertainment and nightlife horizon, and so we set off first to Orlando, to visit a woman who worked for the Disney theme parks and resorts, thinking she might be able to help us out.

From there we went up to Atlanta to visit our old pal and successful entrepreneur Johnny Esposito. Johnny had grown up in Cocoa Beach, but had lived in Atlanta for years. We went to visit a nightclub of Johnny's that was highly successful and unique.

It featured a "big band" sound and swing dancing, but it was all on tape and with no need for an actual 32-piece "big band." The club was hopping and we had a great time listening to the music of another era, but I think at some point both Charlie and I looked at each other and thought, "This is great for a big city like Atlanta, but try selling it to the folks back home."

Who knows? Maybe it would have gone over better than what we tried. Maybe *anything* would have gone over better than what we tried. And what we tried was a little bit of everything that added up to a whole lot of nothing!

"Across the Street"

We called our new venture "Across the Street," for obvious reasons, and billed it as *the* place to go in Cocoa Beach after the sun went down. In advance of our grand opening, we cleaned and scraped and tore down and built up and refurbished and had delivered and pampered and shone the inside and outside until the place looked better than new.

It was a couple thousand square feet of bar space and lounge chairs and brass railings and mirrors and green carpet and hanging plants and boy, it sure looked good.

Like any self-respecting nightclub in the late 70s-slash-early 80s, it featured only the best linoleum dance floor, mirrored walls, light brown paneling, polished brass and green Naugahyde chairs and enough cocktail napkins and swizzle sticks to put the "happy" in happy hour.

We opened the doors in 1977 and you could have heard the crickets chirping from miles away. A lot of my friends showed up, mostly for support and possibly for a free cocktail or two, and it was a great place for Surf employees to go for their shift drink after work, too, but as far as paying customers?

Not so much.

The Nightclub That Was Just Another Bar

Part of it was our fault. You can't just open a nightclub and expect people to come, especially when you have nothing but reasonably priced drinks and a few familiar faces to lure them in. There was no real theme to Across the Street other than, "Bar" or "Lounge".

There wasn't really live music to speak of, no special events, it wasn't a country bar, or a jazz bar or even a gay bar, it was just… a bar. But a really, really big bar with a lot more overhead than Charlie and I expected, and not enough revenue to keep it going for long enough to catch on.

I'm not saying it was a total disaster. Backgammon was big in those days, and we had a nice lounge off to the side with perfectly sized tables for backgammon and other board games.

My old friend Mark Oliver used to come up from Melbourne Beach with his buddies to play backgammon a few nights a week, but who needed to go out to a bar to do that? I always kind of felt he was just being nice to his pal rather than the other way around, but then… I *did* buy a lot of his drinks, so maybe the feeling was mutual!

But that was just the problem: nobody knew what to expect from night to night and month to month, least of all Charlie and myself! Would it be Backgammon night? Or ladies night? What time was Happy Hour? Would there even *be* a Happy Hour? What kind of music was playing? Classic rock or disco?

Feet in the Street: *A Publicity Stunt for the History Books*
(Or, At Least, This Book!)

After a few months of struggling with an empty dance floor and half-empty bar, we hired the Norgren & Davis advertising agency to help promote the nightclub to its target audience. Unfortunately, the guys behind Norgren & Davis were Art Norgren and Ivan Davis, both well into their 70s by the time we retained their services.

They had some great ideas… from Bernard's era of the late 40s and early 50s, that is. Unfortunately, swizzle sticks and cocktail napkins and balloon drops could only go so far in the late 70s and early 80s!

However, I give them credit for one of the best PR stunts I ever saw, and one that many local residents who were around at the time probably still remember to this day.

One day Art and Ivan got it into their heads that having some giant footsteps leading from the front door of Bernard's Surf "across the street" to, well, Across the Street would help lead crowds right into the front entrance. Or at least help them remember the name of the place!

The idea sounded good to me, but good luck getting the Cocoa Beach City Council to approve painting giant footsteps across a busy intersection. Well, never let it be said that Norgren & Davis weren't ingenious.

Art and Ivan found a quick, if vaguely dubious, way around that. By the light of the moon, between 3 and 4 AM one dark Cocoa Beach night-slash-morning, the two elderly gentlemen took some stencils and spray paint and went ahead and did the deed themselves.

With one of them keeping a lookout for late night traffic and/or the cops, who were headquartered just around the corner in those days, the other elderly gentleman bent to the street and spray painted nearly a dozen giant footsteps right across Minuteman Causeway.

To this day I can picture those two old duffers, looking this way and that as they broke – or at least stretched – about a dozen city ordinances to put their covert plan into action. I can also imagine the smile on their faces when they finally looked up, an hour or so later, and saw those big white footsteps "walking" from the Surf to Across the Street.

It worked. You couldn't deny the sight of those giant feet and it made folks curious. Not curious enough to get Across the Street back in black, mind you, but to this day I really think those footsteps are what folks remember most about Across the Street.

I Will Survive

As disco found its way to Brevard County, business gradually picked up for as long as the dancing fad lasted. The dance floor started to fill, the DJ booth got more and more crowded with records – actual vinyl records – featuring Donna Summer, the Village People and Gloria Gaynor.

If Charlie and I were busy before we opened Across the Street, we nearly killed ourselves afterward. 60- and 70-hour weeks, which were bad enough but at least we were used to them, quickly turned into 80- and 90-hour weeks… with no end in sight.

We both took it upon ourselves to personally follow those spray painted footsteps across the street each night after the Surf closed and "check out the scene" at Across the Street.

Okay, so we didn't necessarily *have* to work double and triple shifts five or six nights a week, but as Charlie reminded me not too long ago: we were practically kids ourselves at the time. Both of us were barely in our 30s, and we had the world in our hands back then.

We worked hard and we played hard, were well rewarded financially and if our families had a roof over their heads and warm beds to sleep in while we partied the night away, well then, I think we both thought we were doing "okay" in life.

And, for awhile, I'm proud to say that Across the Street was finally the place to come. The late 70s and early 80s were a weird time in both Cocoa Beach and, I suppose, the country itself. Nightclubs had always been around, of course, but now it was more acceptable than ever to have a few drinks and literally dance the night away, whether it was Saturday night or early Tuesday morning.

On the dance floor, in bell bottoms and clunky heels, you could pass an hour or two – or three or four – and hardly know it. That is, until the bartender suddenly started shouting "last call," turning all the lights on and you looked up to find that it was three or four in the morning!

Folks came and danced and went and danced and told their friends and brought their friends and danced and danced some more. The music flowed and it all sounded the same to me – ask anyone, I've never been a big dancer, although I do all right at weddings – but the people sure seemed to love it, for awhile anyway.

They drank, too, as bar sales finally went up after almost a steady year of losing money. For awhile, it was one of the few successful nightclubs in town, and certainly "the" place to be for a hot minute in the early 80s.

I can remember Norm Kolsch, the longtime owner/manager of the Mouse Trap, fondly regaling me with the following story, which must have happened at the height of Across the Street's popularity:

As they were closing up for the night, two local businessmen asked Norm where the hottest club in town was located. Without thinking much about it, he answered, "Across the Street" and headed them on their way.

Well, ten or fifteen minutes later the gentlemen returned, banging on the door and giving Norm an ear full. Turns out the tourists had taken him at his word and gone literally "across the street" – that is, from the Mouse Trap restaurant.

Locals will recall that, for many years, the only nightclub across from the Mouse Trap was the Evening Edition, the one and only gay bar in Cocoa Beach for years.

In they'd walked, and out they'd walked, red-faced and hot footing it back to the Mouse Trap for directions to the "real" Across the Street, which is what Norm promptly gave them! (After barely containing his laughter, that is.)

It was a great story, and only served to prove my point that, once upon a time, and for a very brief time, Charlie and I had accomplished what we had set out to do: make Across the Street the hot spot we always knew it could be – or at least hoped it *could* be.

Meanwhile, the liquor flowed and the disco music blared and the mirror ball spun and so did our lives, from day to night and night to day and back again. It's all pretty much a blur, to be honest, and cost me a lot of good time with family and friends that I literally didn't have time for in the first place, between the Surf and Across the Street.

About the only good thing to come out of that whole venture was the short shelf-life of disco! Once the music ended around the country, sometime in the early 80s, so too did the fad that had built Across the Street.

The End of An Era, The Beginning of the End

At the end of an cra, we stood at a crossroads. Once the disco phase ended, so did our run as the beach's reining nightclub. You could just feel the lack of business each night when you walked in.

What used to be a thriving dance floor now just looked sad and scuffed from all those disco shoes, and the bar seemed to always be half-empty, no matter the time of day or night.

We tried to make a go of it with a kind of half-stab at renaming Across the Street, "Joker's Wild," but it was just more of the same: a gambling theme without any real gambling, bring back the backgammon and chess boards and the happy hour specials.

It struggled for awhile, until one night my old friend and accountant

Ron Bray approached me with an offer. Our mutual friend, Steve Gray, wanted to buy the place. Ron, having heard me grumble more than a time or two about the business, or lack thereof, knew I wanted to sell and decided to put the two of us together.

At first, I was resistant to the idea. When Ron asked me why, I told him I didn't think it was fair to sell to Steve, who really didn't have a lot of experience in the restaurant and bar business.

I mean, if hardened industry veterans like Charlie and I couldn't make a go of it, actually being in the business, what chance would Steve, who came from a banking background, have?

But Ron finally convinced me to sell. After all, we were all adults and if Steve wanted to buy it, well, all I could do was sign the contract and wish him good luck. I can't remember the exact figure we sold it to him for, but it was around the price I had paid for the building a few years earlier.

Of course, that didn't count the $200,000-plus I'd spent, gambled and lost over those years, from refurbishments and more refurbishments and lost revenue, but the fresh influx of new money didn't hurt and being able to go home at midnight instead of four in the morning didn't hurt, either.

In the end, Across the Street was one of my first, and biggest, misfires as a business owner-slash-entrepreneur and writing this chapter just reminds me of how easy it is to talk yourself into a bad idea.

Unfortunately, it wouldn't be my last…

Chapter 10:

Growing Family, Growing Pains

Every restaurant has growing pains as it gets older, and I suppose you could say the same about restaurateurs. At least, I'm pretty sure you could say the same about me!

I've made my share of mistakes over the years, but I also believe I've learned from each one. Okay, okay, maybe it took me more than a few tries to learn my lesson, but I always learned them, and that's what really counts.

It didn't help matters that shortly after I took over the Surf, I got married, and that shortly after I got married, we had our first son! Running a family business with a growing family led to more growing pains than usual, at home and at work. And, in a family business like Bernard's Surf, it was hard to tell where home began and work ended, or vice versa.

Take Thanksgiving, for instance…

Honey, I Stole the Turkey!

Ask anyone in the restaurant business and they'll tell you that the holidays are a great time to be a customer, and not such a great time to be in the service industry.

Holidays are also a great time for families, except for *our* families! They have to be understanding and recognize how it's our job to make the holidays for other families special, not necessarily our own.

My family has certainly gotten used to the idea of seeing me in fits and starts over the holidays, to this day. And back when I was just starting out in the business I worked every holiday, before, during and after, to make sure that the families who came to the Surf to share their holidays with "our" family had the best dining experience they possibly could.

Oftentimes, this left my own family in the lurch. I can clearly recall, although my first wife Colee recalls it far more clearly, the time I finally did get to spend Thanksgiving Day – the actual day – with the family at home.

There we were, at the dinner table, the 20-pound bird golden and sitting on a platter, all the trimmings decked out around it, from mashed potatoes to green bean casserole to cornbread stuffing when the phone rang.

That… was never a good sign!

Suddenly the whole family tensed, just about to say grace. Like a surgeon on call, I knew it could only be work. Who else would call at dinnertime on Thanksgiving? Sure enough, it was the kitchen, and surprise, surprise, an emergency: they were running out of turkey and still had guests to feed!

I looked at Colee, she looked at me and that was that: On went my suit, and into the restaurant went the bird. It was only twenty pounds but with a little creativity and a LOT of patience, the inspired kitchen staff and I managed to fill the last few orders of the night… with *our* family bird.

It wasn't exactly traditional, but I don't think the family minded when I brought home a few big steaks to serve with the rest of the lonely Thanksgiving side dishes. Still, it was just one example of how folks in the restaurant business have to handle the holidays: one meal at a time.

Another year, not too long after, I was closing up the night before Thanksgiving when one of our regulars, Doug Dederer, just happened to ask me how the turkeys were doing.

In later years we would fine tune our holiday celebration to the point where each table got their own turkey, but back then we just bought several twenty- or thirty-pound birds and carved them up throughout the day.

I was young, just starting out, and maybe Doug just wanted to make sure the holiday went off without a hitch. "They're fine, they're thawing out," I answered, eager to get home after another long night and knowing the next day would be a big one.

Doug gave me a knowing wink and said, "Let's go make sure."

Sure enough, there sat six huge turkeys, frozen solid on the salad room counter. The morning crew was coming in early the next day to cook the birds, but there was no way they'd be ready in time at this rate!

So for the next few hours, Doug and I baby sat those frozen turkeys. We ran water over them, massaged them, yanked out the bags of gizzards and giblets to try and get the birds ready for the day shift the next morning.

It was another late night for a new, young restaurant owner, and of course I rewarded Doug – and myself – with a drink or two. Or three or four. Which is probably when we both got home that night! But what else could I do? If Doug hadn't thought to ask how those birds were doing, who knows what Thanksgiving might have been like that year. As it was, the holiday went off without a hitch, thanks to a little behind the scenes magic in the never boring Surf kitchen.

And as bad – and as long – as that night might have been, it was still preferable to the one Thanksgiving I must have been asleep at the wheel while stocking up in advance of the big day. Instead of ordering 500 pounds of actual turkey, I ordered 500 pounds of... turkey loaf.

The minute it came I knew our gooses were cooked, but by then it was too late to order real turkeys; they were all sold out, everywhere, all over town, in the big grocery chains and the little stores alike. It was the 60s, after all, one of my first Thanksgivings at the Surf and there were no 24-hour Wal-Marts or overnight shipping in those days.

You had what was on stock down the street at the local A & P or you made do with what you had in the walk-in cooler. We had 500 pounds of turkey loaf, and that was what we were stuck with that year.

The folks in the kitchen did the best they could, but there's only so much gravy you can slather on pressed, pre-formed turkey mystery loaf before the customers take note... and tear you a new one!

Hurricanes and Helping Hands

There are lots of benefits to owning a restaurant in Florida. From sunny skies and mostly decent weather to flocks of tourists coming to nearby Orlando and our own sunny beaches and booming space program, it's a great place to run a business – and raise a family.

Then again, there's the occasional gale force winds and destructive path of a hurricane, and that's just what happened when Hurricane

David passed pretty much right along the east coast of Brevard County in September of 1979.

There had been grumblings about evacuation as the storm approached, and then it became mandatory for the beaches and low-lying areas once it was discovered that the storm would reach Category 5 status by the time it made landfall. By then I'd waited a little too long and the consensus in town was that it was safer to stay put than try to cross over one of the bridges heading toward the mainland as the wind gusts were already pretty strong in advance of the approaching storm.

For me, it was just as well. The thought of boarding up the Surf's windows and just letting it stay there, unprotected, felt almost like leaving a family member behind.

So, in the end, we didn't.

Instead, we brought the family to the Surf. With boards on every window – fortunately, there weren't many of them back then – and sturdy 1940s construction in every inch of brick, concrete and mortar, I felt as safe as the policemen and firemen who were staying put just down the street.

So we barreled inside the sturdy back entrance to weather the storm, my family and my brother Ronnie's family, complete with a couple of black Labrador retrievers and plenty of food, water and, of course, enough beer, wine and cocktails to weather several hurricanes.

It was a real hurricane party for awhile there. The adults had their playground, otherwise known as the bar, while the kids had the run of a deserted restaurant, complete with booths, bathrooms, tables, chairs, barstools and waitress stations. And that didn't even include the kitchen which, come to think of it all these years later, was probably not the safest place for a bunch of cooped up kids to play.

With boarded up windows and no sunlight, or moonlight, streaming in, the Surf took on the air of a Vegas casino; time seemed to stand still and in those days before the internet and a 24-hour weather channel, to say nothing of cell phones and Google, we were basically left to determine where the storm was headed by sound alone.

It started as a little rainfall, then a lot, then came the howling, the smashing, the crashing and the train-like sound of 30-, then 40-, then 50-mile per hour winds. And that was just the beginning!

It rained and howled and blew and blew and never stopped blowing, or so it seemed. At one point I was worried I'd made the wrong choice. I think we all were. Well, the adults anyway. Sitting in a deserted dining room, dogs sleeping under the tables, the kids sleeping fitfully, if at all, curled up in leather booths and suddenly you start to think to yourself, "Wow, we're a block from the ocean. What happens if…?"

But the walls held, the roof stayed on and as the eye of the hurricane approached, you could hear the howl turn into a whimper, and then… nothing. Silence. Blissful, complete and utter silence. I'll never forget unlocking the kitchen service door and both of our families crowding onto the delivery platform overlooking the back parking lot and seeing a deserted ghost town.

Wet streets littered with sand and palm fronds and stray pieces of plywood that got knocked off in the storm, but we'd made it. At least, so far. The dogs ran wild after being cooped up for hours on end and so did the kids. Who am I kidding? We all did.

Downtown Cocoa Beach was like a wasteland, the deserted streets looking as if the world had ended and we were the last known survivors. Sand had crept across A1A, covering it with a blanket of dirty white "snow" as the crash of the waves sounded closer than ever. Too close for comfort, you might say.

But the world hadn't ended, and we weren't the only ones in town. So before the hurricane's eye had passed over the center of town completely, we all hustled back inside, lining up tray after tray on every available kitchen counter and filling slices of bread with cold cuts, cheese, tuna and chicken salad before wrapping them all and delivering them personally to the brave policeman and firemen who had stayed behind to weather the storm as well.

It was the least I could do for folks who risked their lives every day, especially during times of tragedy like a Category 5 hurricane. But after a lot of thanks and handshakes all around, it was time to head back to the Surf and lock ourselves in for Round 2 of the storm.

I guess it's fair to say you know the ending to this story, since I'm writing this book, after all. Those who also remained behind and weathered the storm known as David know what I'm talking about when I say I haven't done it since.

Which is not to say it's not a great memory, all things considered. As much time as I've spent inside the Surf over the years, I'll never forget wandering around by candlelight, the power out, the shadows dancing off the walls of the Red Room, flickering behind the bar, realizing I'd instinctively chosen to weather the storm in my business instead of my own home. That my whole family had as well, without question or even a second thought. It said a lot about what the Surf meant to me, what it meant to *them*, and what it still means to this day – if only in distant memories such as these.

Home is the place you want to protect when tragedy strikes, and the place you go when you're in trouble. For the Fischer family, the Surf was more than just a business; it was literally shelter from the storm.

Friends are Family, Too: *The Casbon Family Strikes Again*

Years later, we were having some problems with pilferage in the Dempsey dumpster in the alley behind the Surf. It got bad enough that we had some security cameras installed along the back of the building that would activate whenever something came into view.

I got a call one day from the guy who'd put the cameras in. "I got something," he said, excitedly, after weeks with no progress to report. "I finally got something!" Apparently he had some activity and wanted me to check it out. "Great," I thought, heading over to his office. "We'll finally solve this mystery once and for all."

So I get there and he's got the videotape all set up and we're crouched over his video monitor watching this shaky black and white footage. It's dark out, it's nighttime, it's hard to see, not much light, and nothing going on.

"Here it comes," he kept saying as I watched the lonely dumpster sitting there by itself. "Any second now..." And then, sure enough, a figure came into view. Small and wiry, "a teenager," I thought.

But it was ugly footage and all over very quickly and hard to tell what was really going on. "Play that back for me again, will you?" I asked and we watched the footage once, twice, a couple times more. Each time I saw a little more. It wasn't a teenager after all, but a woman. An older woman, and she wasn't empty handed. She had a bag in hand to take all our recyclables or whatever she'd been pilfering from our trash. But then, the more times I watched, I was pretty sure I knew who it was...and what she was doing.

When I saw the old woman lift up the dumpster lid and toss the bags in for the fourth or fifth time, I stood up and shook my head. "That's just Mrs. Casbon using our dumpsters again," I told him, walking out of the office. We never did find out who was taking stuff out of our dumpsters, but it was no secret who was putting stuff in!

Weekends With Dad (Or Granddad)

Of course, not everything about those earlier years at the Surf were marked by tragedy, turkeys, hurricanes or security cameras. I've been blessed with a satisfying and fulfilling career and, I like to think, my family feels the same about the business that has been such a big part of all of our lives for so very, very long.

Ask any of my kids, and now grandkid, and they'll list the Surf and/ or Rusty's at the Port as among their childhood stomping grounds. For them, it was a big, dark playground full of friendly faces and plenty of hiding places. For me, it was a necessity of the job. You can't work seven days a week, two shifts almost every day, and expect to have a family life if you don't bring the family to work with you once in awhile.

Fortunately, the family never minded too much. Or, if they did, they were sweet enough not to complain! Weekends are generally reserved for family but, in my line of work, I also needed to be around my family business, especially in those early years.

I probably started dragging Rusty Jr. into the bar with me on Sundays when he was just five or six years old. It would be early but the bar would be open, Stan would set "little Rusty" up with a kiddie cocktail and he would sit there in one of the regular barstools, swinging his chubby little legs, happy as a clam as I ran around making sure everything was in order.

Back then the bar had a shelf full of assorted gums and breath mints that I don't think anyone but Rusty Jr. ever noticed anyway, so as long as he got a pack of Juicy Fruit or a roll of Certs, he was happy. Back then a small crowd of regulars would gather in the mornings, Saturdays and Sundays included.

I called them the "breakfast club" and, though the faces changed over the years, they were basically a good group of guys who considered the Surf their home away from home and the bar their church. I couldn't have asked for a better bunch of babysitters as I put out brush fires and occasionally pitched in behind the line or unloading a delivery truck while Little Rusty sat chewing gum and listening to war stories, none the wiser.

As my kids grew, so did their experiences and interfaces with the Surf. Many is the waitress, hostess, cook or salad girl who remembers holding Rusty Jr. or Rhett as kids, or following them around as they hunted down stray kiddie bags in later years.

We couldn't imagine celebrating birthday parties anywhere else, and each year as the kids grew the parties seemed to grow more outlandish. The chocolate covered bees and ants from the Surf's exotic menu were always big hits with the kids, back when we still sold them, and we were lucky to feature our own bakery after awhile, meaning birthday cakes got cheaper to make, and bigger to serve, every year.

It seems in every birthday picture the same red room walls, the same kids, keep showing up, year after year. I hope it was a nice tradition for the kids to be able to hold their birthday parties and other annual celebrations at the Surf every year.

In later years there were disco birthday parties at our nightclub, Across the Street, and as kids got older they were able to bring their prom dates into the Surf, though by then the chocolate covered ants and bees were long gone and the "kids" were more interested in trying to drink underage than scarf birthday cakes or relish trays by the handful.

Later still there were jobs to be had, from summer employment to full-time work to future careers. And now, with my grandson Jack, the habits and routines of over 50 years have come full circle.

Every weekend while he was growing up, Jack and I piled into the car and headed to Rusty's at the Port. There was always money for me to deposit, questions to ask or answer, paperwork to file or forgotten errands to run. And, for Jack, there was always Sprite and maraschino cherries from behind the bar, his own version of a kiddy cocktail, minus the grenadine.

Different kid, different restaurant, but for me it was a habit that was hard to break. I love two things in this world: my family and my family business, and the more I can combine the two, the better.

Even if it is just for a few hours on the weekend...

It All Began With a Margarita:

Notes from a Family Friend

Speaking of family, now is as good a time as any, I figure, to insert the words of close family friend Larry Garrison. I first met Larry in the early 70s, when he was being considered for an administrative position at Cape Canaveral Hospital. We later worked on the hospital board together, and he quickly became a regular at the Surf. More than that, he quickly became a close family friend, someone I'm honored to have known.

Here, then, in his own words, is Larry's story about how the Surf affected his life over the many years he was a patron there:

It began almost four decades ago, well before Bernard's Surf was sold and, eventually, torn down. So much of my professional and personal life was connected to the Surf that many who knew me considered it my "second living room". There is no possible way that I could recount all my special memories – and some misgivings – in one chapter of this book. (It would probably take an entire book of my own!) And besides, if you weren't there, it would probably bore you to tears.

So I have elected to choose a few select highlights over these years to give you a flavor of my experiences at the Surf so that others could share theirs as well:

The Interview

It was April, 1973, and I was applying for the job as Assistant Administrator of Cape Canaveral Hospital. After a formal interview, the Administrator at the time, Ken Wilson, took me to dinner at the Surf. I remember exactly where we sat – the semi-round table on the left as you first entered the main dining area, known to regulars and new guests alike as "the Red Room".

I ordered a margarita and then to my surprise we were served a complimentary filet of the house fried mullet appetizer garnished with a slice of lemon and dollop of homemade tartar sauce. This slice of unexpected generosity was quickly succeeded by an overflowing tray of flat bread – known to regulars as "onion board" – and other assorted rolls and even sweet breads. All that before we were also presented with what the waitress called a "relish tray," which contained an assortment of olives, celery, sweet apple rings and other vegetables.

I could have made a meal out of what the server had already brought us, but – margarita notwithstanding – this was a business meeting, after all, and so I followed Ken's suit and regarded the giant menu while nibbling on my assorted freebies.

The menu was filled with exotic appetizers like buffalo meat and chocolate covered bees. Not taking a chance, I passed on an order of lion's heart (!) and ordered the Doc Stahl's special instead. Crabmeat and shrimp somehow combined to make a fantastic dish. In addition to all the other firsts I experienced that night, it was also the first time I was introduced to the restaurant's owner, and a member of the Hospital Board, Rusty Fischer.

It was a very brief meeting but I was impressed nonetheless by Rusty's insistence on visiting each table personally, and how many of the guests he seemed to know on an intimate and first-name basis. And the best part of all, I got the job!

Employee Recognition Lunch

Up until the 1970s, the hospital had never held a special recognition event celebrating the length of service for employees. Being new to the hospital team, I thought it would be well-received. It was! Rusty was kind enough to let us have a section of the lounge for the inaugural lunch to celebrate long time employees of Cape Canaveral Hospital. If it sounds like an insufficient space to celebrate, keep in mind two things: the hospital was small in those days, so most of the employees being honored could literally fit around the Surf's bar. But most important, they had heard about Bernard's Surf but never dreamed they would ever be able to have lunch there. I'll never forgot how special that day was, honoring people who, themselves, felt honored to be there!

Coming Home

In later years, after a brief stint in administration at Tallahassee Memorial Hospital, I was asked to consider the job as Administrator of Cape Canaveral Hospital. Of course, this second interview was held over dinner at the Surf, down to the same table we'd enjoyed during my first interview.

Only this time, Rusty joined us – along with a couple of other hospital board members and even a few physicians. To conjure up a little of that special magic from my first visit to the Surf, I ordered a margarita and Doc Stahl's special. In due course, I was offered the job.

I said then, "I love this place!"

General Manager

I met Charlie Ragland when I first came to Brevard. Our families attended the same church and we became good friends. At the time, Charlie was manager of the Piccadilly cafeteria at Merritt Square Mall. Always on the search for high caliber talent, Rusty recruited him away to join the Surf management team. It worked well until Charlie went temporarily insane and decided to move to Houston and open his own restaurant.

Unfortunately, it didn't go all that well. So when our hospital Food Service Director retired, I contacted Charlie about his interest in the job and possibly returning to Brevard to take it on. He was excited about the opportunity, so we made travel plans for an interview. Little did I know, there was competition for his services! When I invited Charlie for lunch/dinner following our initial meeting, he politely replied that he was meeting with Rusty "just to say hello"!

Well, that sure was a heck of a hello! Charlie called me the next day to say he was joining the Surf as General Manager. He appreciated the opportunity but he didn't think hospitals were a "good fit" for his particular set of hospitality skills. This time my string of good fortune at the Surf finally ran out. Charlie and I remain close friends to this day, yet you better always be wary of a Seminole!

Sugar Bowl

Every football fan in the South remembers the college season of 1995-1996. FSU had beaten the Gators pretty soundly in Tallahassee at season ending and were headed to the Sugar Bowl for the National Championship. The Gators had only an outside chance unless there was a lot of upsets in other games. That Saturday I spent my entire day at the Surf watching the games. As it unfolded, the upsets happened and the Gators were going to get a rematch with FSU for the National Championship!

Well, I was overly excited – and probably over served – so, very unlike me, I stared opening sugar packets (in honor of the Sugar Bowl, of course) and spreading them all over the Surf lounge. What had I done?! Well, rather than have me ejected on the spot and clean up the mess themselves, the well-trained Surf staff simply brought me a vacuum cleaner and showed me the various electrical outlets to clean up my own mess!

Sure, it was a stupid thing for a grown man to do, but my sugar spreading ritual proved prophetic – we won the rematch and the Gators' first National Championship!

Monday Night Football

Speaking of football, most Monday nights I joined Dan Higgens and Jack Maloy at the Surf bar to watch the game. (Another reason why those who know me considered the Surf my second living room!) Of course, there was some friendly betting involved, which involved the loser buying beer the following Monday.

It seemed an innocuous enough wager and, most Mondays, the "loser" only ended spending twenty or thirty bucks on his friends' beer tab. Well, one Monday night I lost and when I showed up the following week to settle the score, the entire bar – and I mean the entire Surf bar counter – was lined up with beer bottles. I'm not exaggerating when I say there must have been dozens of bottles. I was shocked and asked what happened. Dan and Jack simply reminded me that the Surf opens at 10 AM and they'd been patiently waiting for me to get off work all day!

Breakfast Club

Every Saturday morning, older and mostly retired guys met at the Surf bar for breakfast. Now, the Surf didn't serve breakfast, but the legendary Wanda, the bartender, made it happen once a week nonetheless. Though I considered myself young and was far from retired, I stopped in every now and then and joined them for a Bloody Mary. The gang loved seeing me, if only so they could collectively bitch about hospitals and physicians!

Since there was only one hospital in town back then, what was I going to say? I learned more from them than my weak responses. They talked about many other subjects and I realized their experiences and wisdom was worth the price of a few drinks.

Boss and Friend

For almost forty years as a Board member and Chairman of both Cape Canaveral Hospital and Health First, Rusty was essentially my "boss". He brought to both Boards his business experiences and collaborative manner, which helped in the formative years of Health First. His community involvement was invaluable to hospital management as he shared insights and community needs and issues. Rusty was an excellent sounding board on key matters and his opinion was sought often – and still is to this day.

On a personal basis, I couldn't have a better friend. We were always able to separate boss versus friend and I believe others recognized that and respected it. Rusty is a friend you can trust and love and I am blessed to have made life's journey with him.

Like None Other

Finally, this last section is less of a "story" than pure observation, culled over the (literal) decades I spent in my "second living room".

Rusty and his loyal team created a feel-good environment where everyone could enjoy meeting friends and strangers.

You didn't need to be the astronauts, renowned movie stars, newspaper magnates, bestselling authors, TV personalities or other notables who frequented the Surf to be special. Indeed, Rusty made sure everyone was welcomed and always commented on how much he appreciated their business.

Another special touch was Rusty's ability to recognize so many by name, and greet strangers warmly with a sincere interest in them. It's little wonder why we all returned time and time again, and why first-time customers quickly became "regulars" themselves!

I'm sure I'm not alone when I say thanks, Rusty, for all the memories over the years. You gave myself and hundreds of other "customers" just like me a place to go that was, truly, like a second home. From the friendly and faithful staff to the inviting atmosphere to the familiar menu to the generously poured drinks, you turned meals into memories and guests into family.

I'm honored to be one of them!

Scenes from an Opening Night
Bob Grothe, the Surf's very first manager and my original mentor, Tom Gavin,
Tony "Two Ton" Galento, Bernard Fischer and Herb Dawley, posing playfully
behind the bar on opening night in 1948.
[Author's Collection]

The Roaring 50s
Bernard's Surf started as a cocktail lounge in the late 1940s and, several
years later when this picture was taken, business was officially booming.
It would later expand into a restaurant that would launch the careers of
three generations of "Fischer Men"! [Author's Collection]

A Well-Stocked Bar
A nattily attired bartender, not Bernard, for once, shaking, not stirring, a drink
for someone at the crowded Surf bar, circa the 1950s. [Author's Collection]

Behind the Bar
Bernard at his finest, serving a thirsty guest a fancy drink as he toiled
alongside bartender Herb Dawley, circa the 1950s. [Author's Collection]

Good Food, 'Nuff Said
The Surf as it looked in the very beginning: small, local and
convenient. The lot might have been unpaved, but inside the
menus featured delicacies from all over the world!

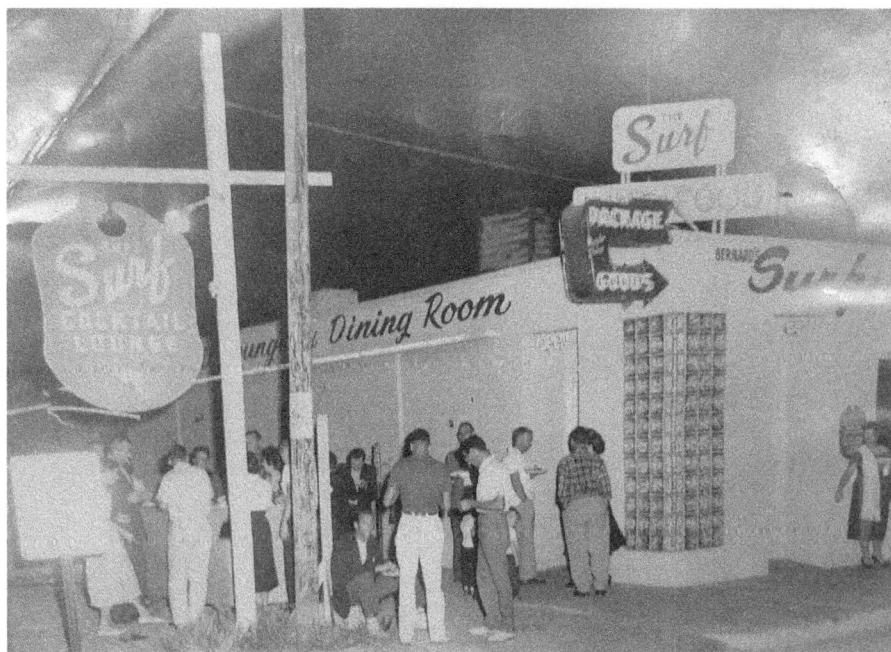

Standing Room Only
A vintage scene from one of the earliest Surf anniversary parties, circa
1950-something, featuring a spillover crowd feasting on free steamed
shrimp in the parking lot! [Author's Collection]

Standing Room Only 2

More of the spillover crowd from a standing room only anniversary celebration on Halloween, circa 1950-something, at Bernard's Surf. Or, at least, beside it!
[Author's Collection]

The Surf Postcard

A vintage postcard featuring the exterior and interior of Bernard's Surf cocktail lounge and dining room as it appeared in its earliest incarnation. The exterior still looks fairly isolated, but in later years the Surf would be at the heart of a booming downtown Cocoa Beach, no longer an island unto itself! [Author's Collection]

Progress in Black and White
Bernard's Surf as it looked in what appears to be the late 1950s: far
removed from the corner bar it started as, but not quite the space age
landmark it was destined to become! [Author's Collection]

Casual Bernard
Most people have only seen my uncle, Bernard Fischer, in a business
suit holding a Surf menu, but this is the photo that hangs over my desk,
a constant reminder of the man who started it all. [Author's Collection]

Dressed to the Nines

A vintage photo of Uncle Bernard and his Surf staff, complete with a full-time chef and waitresses in formal attire. (Good luck getting the Rusty's crew to dress like this every night! Can you say "mutiny"?) [Author's Collection]

Working the Floor

Uncle Bernard, in his best suit and (bow) tie, doing what he did best – working the floor – in a crowded Surf dining room circa the 1950s. [Author's Collection]

BEER & ALE

Premium Beer and Ale (Domestic)	.45
Country Club	.45
Champale	.45
Lowenbrau (Germany)	.75
Heinekins (Holland)	.65
Bass Pale Ale (England)	.90
Guines Stout (England)	.80

ON DRAUGHT

Michelob		Small	.20
½ Yard	1.00	Med.	.40
Yard	1.50	Large	.75
Lowenbrau (Germany)		Small	.40
½ Yard	2.00	Med.	.80
Yard	3.00	Large	1.50

SATURN

(For Four)

Sparkling Catawba, Grape Juice,
Vodka, Lemon, Cordial

$8

APOLLO

GALLIANO, VODKA
and LIME JUICE
ON THE
ROCKS
1.75

Bottoms Up!
Bernard's Surf beer menu (circa 1950-something) featuring a wide range
of foreign and domestic beers, including Lowenbrau (remember them??)
for 75 cents, Heineken for 65 cents and our famous yard of beer filled
with Michelob for a whopping $1.50!!! [Author's Collection]

119

A Menu to Behold (With Both Hands!)
One of the peak vintage menus from my vast collection, featuring a few of the
Surf's accolades at the time, including being included in Gourmet magazine. In the
top right corner, you can see where these menus were available for purchase, all
proceeds contributing to the "new" Cape Canaveral Hospital.

Every Order Cooked To Order -- Please Have P
We Will Do Our Utmost To Please

Bernard Fischer
Proudly Presents

PAN FRIED

ABALONE STEAK

Bernard Fischer
Proudly Presents

BAKED

DANISH LOBSTER

EN CASSEROLE

Bernard Fischer
Proudly Presents

BROILED FILET

OF

Bernard Fischer
Proudly Presents

BROILED

GENUINE ENGLISH

VER SOLE ALMONDINE

of Potato, Salad or Soup

OT BREAD & BUTTER

ian Lobster Cocktail

BUTTER
ard
oudly

Ranch Cut Steak
dinner includes
A large portion of prime black angus sirloin carved
and served in a manner reminiscent of the old west.
Choice of Potato, Choice of Salad,
Hot Breads and Butter, Coffee or Tea
served in kettle steak
whenever possible. $4.95 per person

*Baked Giant Shrimp
Stuffed with
Fresh Fla. Crabmeat
In
Garlic Wine Sauce
4.50*

*Above entrees served
with
Choice of Potato, Salad
or Soup
Hot Bread & Butter
Coffee or Tea*

Kangaroo Steaks in Wine Sauce (Australia)   10.00
Kangaroo Tail Soup (Australia)   2.50
Barbecued Quails on Skewers (Japan)   1.95
Alligator Soup   3.50
Birds Nest Soup (England)   2.25
Sharks Fin Soup (England)   2.50
Cream of Snails Soup (Germany)   2.25
Norwegian Reindeer Steak
  in Madeira Wine Gravy   3.95

Bernard's Surf
Cocktail Lounge and Dining Room
COCOA BEACH, FLORIDA
Recommended By Gourmet
Member
Diners Club — American Express Co.
Hiltons Carte Blanche

ALL YOU CAN EAT
French Fried Canaveral

A BOWL FULL
of
Cold Steamed

SHRIMP

Inside, you can see the handwritten daily specials and variety of seasonal dishes on offer at the time, including English Dover Sole Almondine and Pan Fried Abalone Steak. [Author's Collection]

Liftoff With These Vintage Drink Menus

A panoramic view of our drink menus from the same time period (mid-1950s)
featuring a variety of our space-themed cocktails, ranging from the "Moon Shot"
(151-proof rum, vodka and cream) to the "Titan" (190-proof alcohol, 151-proof
rum and green chartreuse) and my personal, if confusing, favorite "The Blue
Scout," featuring a "fine cognac and a fine Havana cigar" for just $1.50!!

[Author's Collection]

Brotherly Love
My brother Ronnie and I, seated for our "official" portrait, circa 1944. Hard
to believe I was such a young tyke only a few years before the Surf opened,
only to call it my own a few short decades later! [Author's Collection]

"Let's Go!"
The author as I must have looked around the time of the infamous transistor
radio rebellion in the Melbourne High auditorium on the morning of the historic
Alan Shepard launch in 1951, buzz cut and Madras shirt and all. "Let's go!"
[Author's Collection]

The Fischer Men
A historic portrait of the four original "Fischer-men" that now hangs in the foyer of
Rusty's at the Port: my uncle Sydney Fischer (standing, in the red shirt and glasses),
my father Lou beside him and, kneeling from left to right, Uncles Ed and Bernard.
[Author's Collection]

Fischer Pier
The old Fischer pier, somewhere in the late 1930s to early 1940s, located
on the south side of the cape before the Port was officially Port Canaveral.
[Author's Collection]

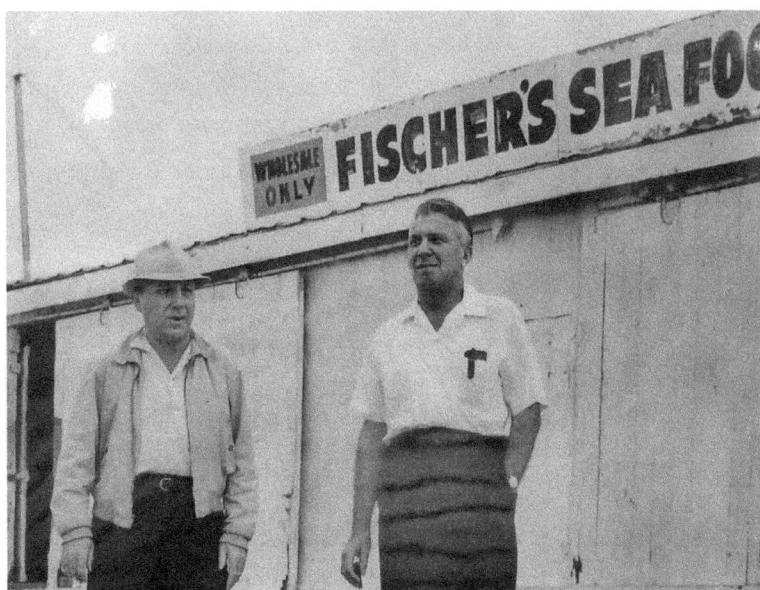

Fischer's Seafood
My father, Lou Fischer, and his brother Eddie looking nautical – and
nostalgic – in front of the old Fischer's Seafood warehouse at Port Canaveral.
[Author's Collection]

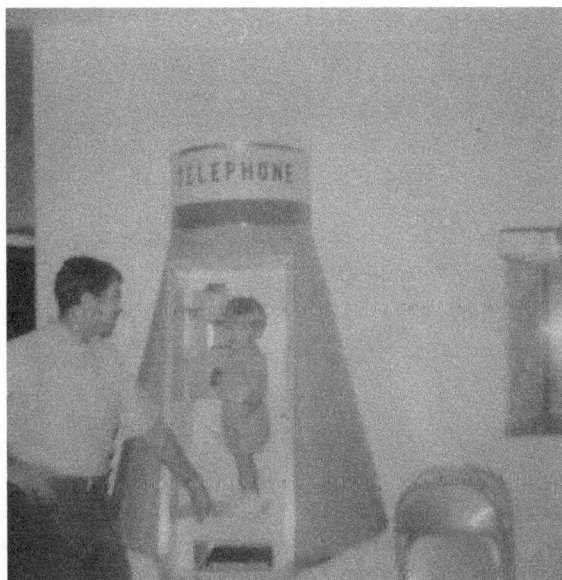

Space Everything, In Every Space
Ah, the late 1960s, where even the phone booths in Cocoa Beach were space-
themed! Here is Rusty Jr. playing astronaut in a play space capsule-slash-phone
booth, no doubt calling the moon… collect! [Author's Collection]

A Hero's Welcome!
An oddly familiar sight back in the 1960s in Cocoa Beach, astronauts receiving a
Hero's Welcome, not just from an adoring crowd of Space Coast residents – but
from babes in bikinis! [Author's Collection]

History Repeating Itself
John Glenn's triumphant return to space aboard space shuttle Discovery
in 1998 was celebrated by recreating (as closely as possible) his original
ticker tape parade through Cocoa Beach over three decades earlier in 1962!
[Author's Collection]

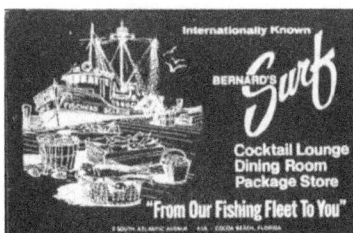

Internationally known

A promotional postcard featuring the Surf's familiar slogan, "From our fishing fleet to you." More than just a catchy marketing phrase, the Fischer fleet of boats was, at one time, one of the largest on the Eastern coast. [Author's Collection]

Souvenirs from a Distant Era

A sampling of some of the souvenir glasses we'd give out for the Surf's anniversary party every Halloween, along with some assorted stir sticks and, of course, the Surf's famous matchbooks. I should hold onto these – matchbooks just like them are going for nearly $20 on eBay these days! [Author's Collection]

Faded Memories
This faded 1948 menu from Bernard's Surf features an "imported sardine" sandwich for 85 cents and all you can eat "French Fried Canaveral Jumbo Shrimp" for $2.50! It's amazing, considering the size of the Surf kitchen back then, how they were able to create such a symphony of flavors with so little space and resources! [Author's Collection]

South of the Borders
A bruised and battered Surf menu from a bygone era, with borders full of daily specials, hand applied by loyal staff members like Juli Shroble and featuring everything from Stone Crab Legs (far more plentiful in those days), to Frog Legs to Chicken Livers and Mushrooms to South Carolina Squab! [Author's Collection]

APPETIZERS
Choice of
Cold Conaveral Shrimp
Indian River Crab Claws
Florida Key's Stone Crab Claws

Relish Tray Assorted Bread Basket
Choice of Soup or Salad
Crab Bisque Tossed Garden Salad
Onion Soup Choice of Dressing

WINES
B & G Pouilly Fuisse - 1971
B & G Medoc - 1971

ENTREES
ROAST PRIME RIBS OF BEEF, Au Jus
Served with Horseradish Sauce
BERNARD'S SPECIAL FILET MIGNON
Served with Sauteed Mushrooms and Wild Rice
BROILED FLORIDA LOBSTER TAILS
Served with Drawn Butter
FRIED SHRIMP, A LA RUTH
Seasoned with Cheese, Garlic and Lemon
FRIED SNAPPER, A LA DORIS
Prepared with Seasoned Breadcrumbs

Choice of Potato or Vegetable with all entrees

CHOICE OF DESSERTS
Tangy Florida Key Lime Pie
Creme De Menthe Parfait

COFFEE ... TEA
After Dinner Cordials

ХОЛОДНЫЕ ЗАКУСКИ
Выбор:
Холодные канаверальские креветки
Клешни крабов из Индиан Ривер
Клешни крабов с флоридских островов
Салатные Заправки Хлеб
Суп или салат на выбор
Суп молочный с крабами Салат из свежих овощей
Луковый суп Соусы для салата
ВИНА
Пулли Фуис - 1971 /полусладкое/
Медок - 1971 /сладкое/
ГОРЯЧИЕ БЛЮДА
Котлета говяжья натуральная на косточке
под соусом /с хреном/
Филе миньон по бернардовски
/с жареными грибами и рисом/
Жареные вейки флоридского лангуста
/с растопленным маслом/
Креветки жареные, "а ла руть"
/заправленные сыром, чесноком и лимоном/
Снаппер жареный, "а ла дорис"
/в сухарях/
Гарнир по выбору - картофель или овощи
по всем горячим блюдам
ДЕССЕРТ ПО ВЫБОРУ
Лимонный кекс из флориды
Наполеон "Крем де мент"
кофе, чай
ликеры и напитки

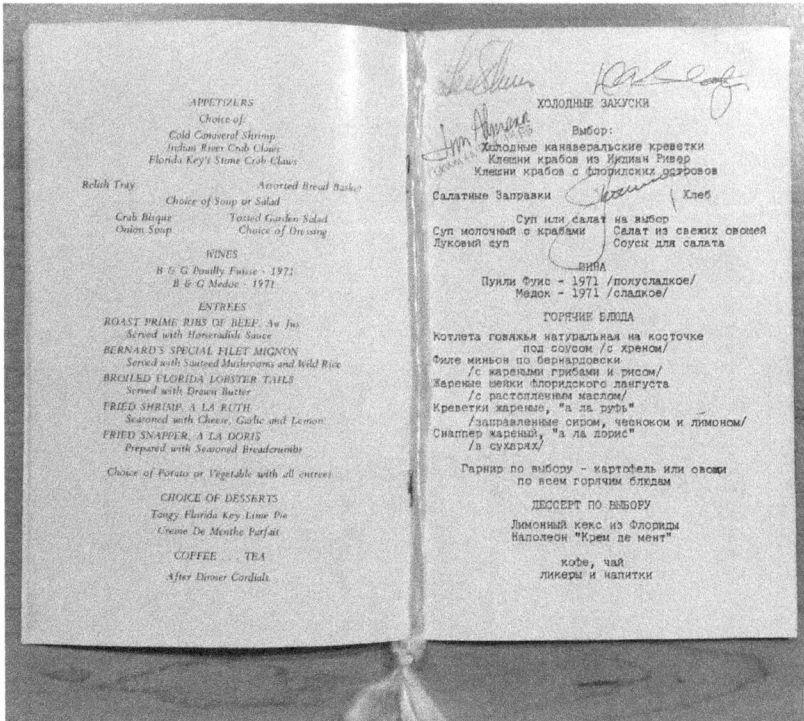

Multilingual
The inside of the Apollo-Soyuz menu featuring the specially selected items in both English and Russian, bearing some of the many signatures of those brave astronauts and cosmonauts from the original 1975 mission. [Author's Collection]

Then and Now: Apollo Soyuz
Me pouring champagne for the American astronauts and Soviet cosmonauts in
honor of the original Apollo Soyuz Test Project mission in 1975 versus me sharing
a drink with the same brave men 15 years later in a follow-up (and much more
relaxed) 1990 celebration! [Author's Collection]

Souvenirs from Space
Soyuz mission commander Alexei Leonov drew this version of the linked space vessels, mid-flight, while autographing one of the regular Surf menus! To this day, it's one of my most treasured possessions. [Author's Collection]

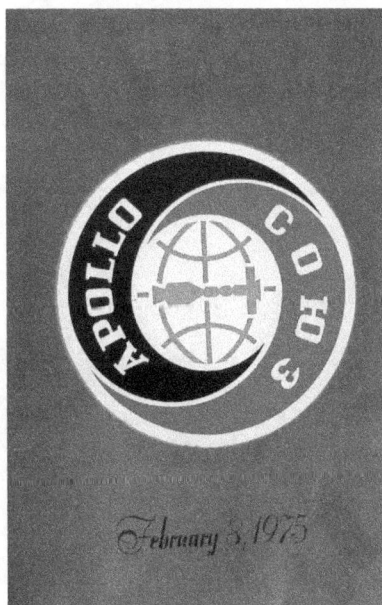

Soyuz Menu
The cover design of the special menu featured to commemorate the historic Apollo Soyuz Test Project on February 8, 1975. [Author's Collection]

French Wine for the Russian Cosmonauts, Oh Well, Go Get 'Em Charlie!
That feeling when you may have slightly ordered the wrong vintage so you send
your General Manager (and general partner in crime) out to pour a glass of (French)
champagne for the (Russian) cosmonauts in advance of their 1975 mission.
[Author's Collection]

A Fairly Formal Affair
Even as the 70s raged on, the Surf still clung to a fairly formal attire for its wait
staff. Here is a great "slice of life" picture from Juli Shroble that takes me back to a
random night shift during the Surf's heyday! [Courtesy of Juli Shroble]

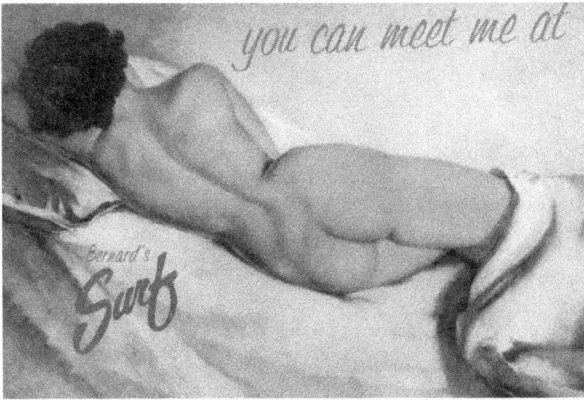

You Can Meet Me At...
A postcard of the infamous painting that hung behind the bar for decades in Bernard's Surf, launching thousands of urban legends about where it might have come from and who it might be... and just as many fantasies! [Author's Collection]

Friendship Never Fades
Photos may fade, as this one has over time, but not friendships, like the one I have with the young fella in this photo, Bill Hammond. [Author's Collection]

Bo Pete
No book about Bernard's Surf would be complete without a
candid photo of Bo Pete! [Author's Collection]

Good Old Charlie
My longtime general manager and, ultimately, close personal friend, Charlie
Ragland, proudly presenting a photo collage from the original 1975 Soyuz-Apollo
dinner during our more relaxed 1990 reunion with some astronauts/cosmonauts.
[Author's Collection]

Rhett in the Red Room
Me listening patiently as my youngest son (and future co-owner), Rhett,
details his plans for the future of the company!!! [Author's Collection]

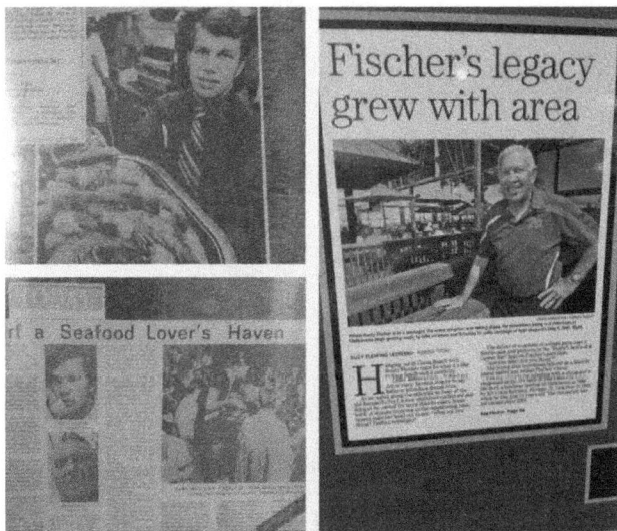

Then and Now: Florida Today
Myself in an early story for Florida Today from the 1960s and a more
recent Florida Today article about the Fischer legacy in Brevard. It's been
a wild ride, but I've been fortunate to not only be a part of the Space Coast
community, but be embraced by them as well! [Author's Collection]

Three Restaurants in One
The Surf as it looked in the mid-1980s, featuring not one, not two but three different and unique restaurants in one: the original Bernard's Surf (including the "Red Room" and original dining room), Fischer's Lounge (what was the original Surf Bar) and the all-new Rusty's Raw Bar. The blue and white exterior was designed to match the blue and white uniforms of the "Rusty's Girls"! [Author's Collection]

Remains of the Day
The original Surf façade as it appeared during the bittersweet demolition of the crumbling structure in 2018. The old building might be gone, but the spirit of Uncle Bernard and his legacy of fresh seafood and family dining live on… at Rusty's at the Port! [Author's Collection]

Fischer's Seafood
A glimpse into the past, at the original building that was later to house Rusty's Seafood & Oyster Bar. Originally, brother Ronnie ran the seafood market, bait store and ticket center for his deep sea fishing charter boat, The Miss Cape Canaveral, out of this very building. [Courtesy of Ronnie and Ryan Fischer]

Miss Cape Canaveral
Here, in all its faded glory, is the Miss Cape Canaveral, chugging back into Port after a long day at sea. Loaded with fishing aficionados, it's passing the old Rinker silos, still visible in most of the Rusty's social media pics to this day! [Courtesy of Ronnie and Ryan Fischer]

Rusty's Girls
You've heard of the "Bond Girls," well... here are the Rusty's Girls! A publicity
photo from the early 90s when we opened Rusty's at the Port, which the staff fondly
(and some not-so-fondly) refer to as the "blue short" days! [Author's Collection]

Alan B. Shepard Jr.

From Auditorium to Autograph
Once upon a time I watched Alan Shepard become the first American in space,
from the grassy fields behind Melbourne High. In later years I would welcome
this living legend into my own restaurant, shake his hand and get his autograph.
This picture, one of my prized possessions, hangs to this day in the lobby of
Rusty's at the Port, part of a mini-museum of sorts in tribute to my days living
on, and working on, the Space Coast! [Author's Collection]

Official Portrait
The "official portrait" of Uncle Bernard looking spiffy and dapper in a
three-piece suit and holding a Surf menu that still hangs prominently
today at Rusty's at the Port. [Author's Collection]

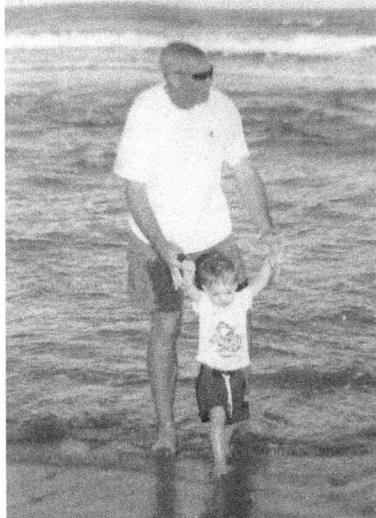

A Grandfather at Last!
Good times with my grandson Jack, frolicking in the waves on the same
beach where I'd trained for the Junior Olympics way back in the 1950s!
[Author's Collection]

Liftoff!!
I sure do miss the Surf, but there's something to be said about watching
a midday launch go off from your upstairs office! Enjoy the view…
from Rusty's at the Port!! [Author's Collection]

Same as it ever was…
Where once the day crew and I would step outside the Surf doors to watch a
launch sail out over Space Coast skies, now the Rusty's crew posts up on the roof
to watch a SpaceX launch, live and in person – and closer than ever. The more
things change, the more they stay the same… [Author's Collection]

Location, Location, Location...
As if the cruise ships sailing past a crowded deck weren't enough, Rusty's at the
Port is blessed with being located right across from the SpaceX fleet of operations,
where we see scenes like this one, a flame-scorched rocket booster returning to Port,
unfold on a (thankfully) regular basis. [Author's Collection]

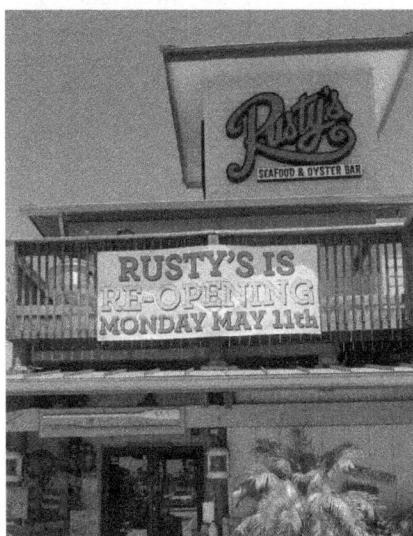

Scenes from a Pandemic
Like many restaurants around the country, Rusty's at the Port had to shut down
for over a month due to Covid-19. Here we are anxiously awaiting our grand
"reopening," and uncertain about how guests would react to dining out again.
Fortunately, they came back out – in droves! [Author's Collection]

Cruising Toward the (Uncertain) Future
As of this writing, the cruise industry is tentatively getting back on its (sea) legs, meaning scenes like this one will eventually – hopefully – get back to normal. Bon voyage... from Rusty's at the Port!! [Author's Collection]

Chapter 11:

Walk of Fame

While astronauts deserve a Walk of Fame of their own, there have been many other famous faces who've visited Bernard's Surf over the years. Most of them, unsurprisingly, were there because of the space program, adding to the nostalgia of a bygone era that now only belongs to the history books and my own faded memories:

"And That's the Way It Is…"

When it comes to my favorite famous people, Walter Cronkite is right up there at the top of the list. While I'd hardly have called us friends, the journalism legend was certainly friendly over the years and made a lasting impression on me that remains, warm and familiar, to this day.

Cronkite first visited the Surf in the 60s and 70s where, as a fresh-faced reporter who even then wore his trademark thick, black glasses, he was reporting on the early days of the space program.

While most people picture Cronkite as a staid and calm fellow as he read the nightly news for countless years on our family televisions across the country, I remember a slightly different celebrity when the cameras were off and the (dry, endlessly witty) jokes were flying.

The space program was a specific time and place in our country's history, and those brave astronauts both lived and played hard. They liked a good joke, a funny prank and a risky dare as well as any other pilot, I suppose, and then some because they were, after all, pilot's pilots.

To write about them as subjects of countless news stories, the reporters who covered the astronauts had become like familiar pals to those of us at the Suf. And it was with respect and admiration that

I watched Cronkite and his fellow journalists interact with these living legends as they mingled in the busy cocktail lounge in the days preceding a big launch.

Walter could laugh and tell stories with the best of them, and had a dry wit that was always so surprising coming from his unassuming appearance. With his sleeves rolled up and his press pass buried deep in his shirt pocket, Cronkite could be just another one of the guys. I always got the feeling he kind of enjoyed his trips to the Space Coast, and hopefully Bernard's Surf as well.

My longtime manager and close friend Charlie Ragland recalls just how dry Cronkite's humor could be with a story that never fails to make me smile. Before Charlie joined the Surf he was a hotshot young corporate type for the Piccadilly cafeteria chain.

As he recounted the story to me, during a sales retreat in the Bahamas, Charlie was coming back up from the beach to crash in his hotel room for the night. Drunk enough to stumble but sober enough to recognize a familiar face, who did he spot just outside the hotel lobby but the man, the legend himself: Walter Cronkite.

"Walter!" Charlie was just buzzed enough to shout, approaching the living legend as if the two were old friends.

Mr. Cronkite, polite as ever, turned and offered him a friendly, if cautious, smile. "Do I know you, sir?" he asked, as anyone might after being accosted by a loud, boisterous type in, if I know Charlie, an even louder Hawaiian shirt.

"Walter," Charlie said, laying it on thick with a disappointed face. "You come into my living room every night at 6 PM and you still don't remember me *yet*?"

Cronkite had a chuckle over a joke he must have heard a dozen times that day already, and countless times in his lifetime. Charlie let him off the hook with a hearty laugh before promptly passing out in his bed, never imagining he'd get the chance to meet the man again.

Fast forward to just a few years later and there's Charlie, managing the Surf as another launch prepares to go off. Cronkite comes in, friendly as ever, quiet and unassuming. Charlie bides his time, sure the living legend would never remember the encounter.

Not wanting to appear rude, he did as he always did with celebrities or other dignitaries. He quietly and quickly approached the table to acknowledge Cronkite, let him know who he was and also let him know if he needed anything, he was the man to ask.

Maybe it was Charlie's booming voice or his smiling face, but either way Cronkite studied him carefully, and for longer than he needed to.

"Do you recognize me, sir?" Charlie couldn't help but ask, if a little sheepishly.

"It's coming to me," Cronkite nodded, before smiling and delivering yet another of his famous punch lines. "Now I've got it: you're that drunk from the Bahamas!"

With a boisterous laugh and a good-natured blush, Charlie had to admit he'd been caught; the man was right. Telling me the tale the next day, Charlie had an air of pride as he concluded, "Coming from a guy like Cronkite, I'll take that as a compliment."

Hiding in Plain Sight

In 1998 John Glenn was scheduled to go back into orbit on the space shuttle Discovery, becoming the oldest man to ever fly in space. For a man who had first launched into space decades earlier, this wasn't just local news, or even national news – it was *global*. Naturally, the most distinguished name in broadcast news was front and center on the story: Walter Cronkite himself.

It just so happened that John Glenn's launch was scheduled the week of the Surf's 50th Anniversary celebration! Needless to say, the Surf was THE place to be that week amidst the flurry of parades, press conferences and star gazing that had invaded our normally quiet coastal town.

This being the week of Halloween, my longtime assistant and PR person extraordinaire, Jane Vester, had scheduled a costume contest as just one of the many events designed to celebrate the Surf's 50th year in business. The contest was being held in the back parking lot, where a stage had been set up and an announcer was inviting all the contestants up to show off their most creative costumes.

Cronkite was inside the Surf lounge, far away from the maddening crowd enjoying a brief break from all the reporting and story filing he was in the midst of that week. I always tried to stay low key around celebrity types as a rule, but it was a big week for us and, after a shot or two – or perhaps three or four – of courage, I approached Walter and reminded him about the costume contest.

"Wouldn't it be something," I suggested half-heartedly, never imagining he'd actually take the bait, "if you went out there and joined the contest... dressed as yourself?"

He slid his glasses down his nose a little and offered me that trademark chuckle, before politely declining. *Oh well,* I thought to myself as I returned to the contest, slightly embarrassed. *Nothing ventured, nothing gained.* But even so it wasn't long after that that Walter Cronkite got up and went out the back entrance, sticking around and watching the costume contest for over an hour.

I'll never forget how casual, friendly and approachable he looked that night. Shoulder to shoulder with everyday folks like you and I, he "oohed" and "aahed" and clapped and cheered the night's big winners before slipping into the night, back to his life as a living legend.

The Thriller

Vincent Price is certainly still considered a legend today, but in the late 60s and all throughout the 70s he was like living royalty. An international superstar known mainly for his roles in such popular horror movies as *The Pit and the Pendulum, House on Haunted Hill, The Tingler* and *House of Wax*, Price was also a globe-trotting bon vivant who enjoyed the finer things in life. (He was also a giant of a man, seriously. I'm no slouch and when he stood to greet me, he towered over me!)

When he and his wife, Mary Grant Price, were in town, a restaurant like Bernard's Surf was right up their alley. Cocktails and appetizers and relish trays and bread baskets and long, lingering dinners in a cozy leather booth were clearly what the fab couple were used to, and I'll never forget the honor Mr. Price paid me when he tapped one of our oversized dinner menus during one such lavish meal and stated, "This menu is fantastic."

Hearing that world famous voice say those words was a thrill I'll never forget. Colee, my wife at the time, was an avid cookbook collector and it just so happened she had the cookbook that Vincent and his wife had written together, *A Treasury of Great Recipes* (Ampersand Press, 1965).

Now, much like the Surf menu was over the top in its lavish amount of menu items and lion heart and chocolate covered ants, the Prices' cookbook is as much about their lavish lifestyle as it is the art of cooking. Filled with lush pictures from their jet setting adventures, Colee couldn't get to the Surf fast enough when she heard Vincent Price and his wife were there.

The minute she got there she lugged the beast of a giant cookbook over to their table and breathlessly asked both Mr. and Mrs. Price to sign it for her. When the couple heard we would soon be visiting Cape Cod over the summer, Mrs. Price flipped to a page in the cookbook that featured a wonderful little inn that she said we just "had to try." The picture showed a quaint and charming, rustic inn with Vincent and Mary Price standing in front of it.

Sure enough, a few months later when we were in fact tooling around Cape Cod, nothing would do but we find the same inn, eat there and recreate the picture ourselves!

I share this story not only because of my respect for a talented man like Vincent Price and his equally talented wife, but for the pride I always felt when a true gourmet took the time to order something truly delicate and complicated from the menu, wait patiently for it to be prepared and then let me know how much he or she liked it.

Getting a nod of approval from a gourmand like Vincent Price himself was well worth all the time and effort my uncle Bernard took to create a menu that he liked to brag was "internationally famous."

I always kind of thought it was a stretch as far as slogans went, but in such moments as these, I even started believing it myself!

Just Another Launch Night...

Back in the heyday of the space program, when launches were more or less "common" for those of us living and working on the Space Coast, you never know who you might see walking into the Surf on a random weeknight, especially when a launch might be in the near distant offing.

One thing I can say about Al Neuharth, if I haven't already said enough, is that he was good for business. Thanks to his connections in the newspaper industry and with big media, I can honestly say that Al brought in pretty much every major and even not-so-major journalist, reporter and particularly news anchor that was popular in the 60s, 70s, 80s and beyond.

We're talking everybody, from David Brinkley to Peter Jennings to Walter Cronkite to Dan Rather to Tom Brokaw. I can't tell you the number of times I looked up from washing a fresh beer glass or pouring a shot to see a famous newscaster looking back at me, Al Neuharth standing proudly at his side and ready to make the introductions.

I'll never forget the night I sat down next to John Chancellor, who rivals Walter Cronkite as one of my favorite all-time reporters and, later, famous newscasters. It was late on yet another launch night, but the crowd was thinning and he didn't seem to mind the company. (Or, if he did, didn't have the heart to shoo me away.)

You can always tell what kind of person a celebrity is – what kind of a person they *really* are – by how they act when they're sitting at a bar, sleeves rolled up, tie loosened, the camera off… just one of the guys, away from the lights and adoring fans.

John Chancellor was one of the guys. He was smart, friendly, kind and gracious. We talked about the space program that night, how could we not? But to Mr. Chancellor's credit, we talked about a lot of other things as well.

He asked about the restaurant, the beach, and he seemed to understand that life went on after he and his reporter friends were gone and it was just the regulars and tourists sitting at the bar in their place. I had many moments like that over the years, with folks famous and anonymous alike, about life in the town where the rockets went up.

But that was one of my favorites…

In Which I Make a Better Quarterback Than a Defensive Lineman

Walter "Wally" Schirra was one of the original hardcore, old-school astronauts. I mean, this guy was a living legend in a time of real living legends. Not only was he one of the original seven astronauts chosen for the Mercury Program, but as I understand it he is the only man to fly in all three of first three space programs: the Mercury, Gemini and Apollo missions.

He was also just one hell of a good guy and a common enough face at the Surf during the heyday of the space program. Now, for those who didn't grow up around rockets and the (mostly) men who flew them, let me just tell you that they are babe magnets. Equal parts athlete, rocket scientist, rock star and celebrity, these guys couldn't avoid the ladies if they tried. (And, from what I could see, they rarely tried.)

But Walter was a gentleman and discreet enough as far as these things went, and I understood his need for as much privacy as he could get when he was in town on the down low, which often happened before or especially after a big mission.

I can remember one night a certain reporter was angling for information on the whereabouts of Walter, and kept calling to ask me if I knew if he was in town and, if so, where he might be. Now, this guy knew that, eventually, one or more of the astronauts would more than likely make it to Bernard's Surf.

Not to sound cocky, it was just part of the "circuit" as they made their way around town between launches, from the Mouse Trap to Wolfie's Lounge to Ramon's to the Surf and back to the Holiday Inn... where I hear the real party started. (But that's another story, for another book!)

On this particular night, the only reason I might have known a celebrity was in the house was because of the sudden appearance of a bevy of beautiful young women dressed to the nines and looking for trouble.

Sure enough, I spotted Wally at one of the Surf lounge's stand-up tables, surrounded by a couple young ladies who seemed very eager for his take on polycarbonate retrofittings! (Or maybe not...) Now, lots of the astronauts were married men with loving families back home, but that rarely stopped the "rocket groupies" from zeroing in on them whenever they were in town. In my experience, while always polite to these local ladies, the astronauts themselves were as loyal to their spouses as they were to their commitment to being the "best of the best". Mr. Schirra was no exception to this rule.

Only minutes later the reporter who'd been pestering me all day walked in and aimed himself at me like a rocket veering off the launch pad. I did what any self-respecting restaurant owner in the same situation would do: put myself strategically in between Wally and the reporter.

After all, no celebrity is going to keep going back to the same restaurant if the minute he shows up the owner calls the press and lets them know he's in town.

Unfortunately, I was always the quarterback and never the defensive lineman and, for whatever reason, the more I tried to protect poor Wally, the more I must have given him away with a slight tick or a nervous glance!

Either way, the reporter was no dummy.

"Is Wally Schirra here?" he finally asked, point blank.

"No," I lied.

He smirked, ran a blitz around my left flank and sure enough, Wally was toast; the guy was all over him like a tight space suit in a cramped capsule.

Hey, I tried!

Where Everybody Knows Your Lawsuit

I'm fairly proud to say that the Surf and, in later years, Rusty's at the Port both became and stayed popular without the help of a ton of advertising. Sure, we do the usual newspaper coupons and special holiday ads and drink specials like most restaurants, but you don't hear a ton of radio spots about us and you certainly don't see many TV commercials, either. (This chapter may explain why!)

Well, all that changed in the 1990s when a local ad agency finally talked me into filming a TV commercial for the Surf. I only agreed because the concept was so good. Anyone who's ever been to the Surf more than once or twice knows that you'll see the same faces on most occasions, usually seated around the bar in the Surf lounge. (Or as my kids, who grew up in the days of the Raw Bar "downstairs" call it, the "Adult" bar.)

Well, the concept for the commercial was simple: have me standing behind the bar, doing my best "Sam Malone" impersonation, and as one regular after the other comes in, we call out their names:

"Hey, George!"

"Hey, Randy!"

"Hey, Bill!"

Whatever. It was quick, simple, easy to set up and shoot and we all thought it would make a good case for the Surf as your friendly, neighborhood lounge and restaurant, where "everybody knows your name."

Obviously, that's who we were copying at the time, the famous "Cheers" tag line, but I guess we all figured, who would watch a little old TV commercial about a little old family restaurant in little old Cocoa Beach, Florida, right?

Well, someone did, and fast, because only a week or two after the commercial began airing on local television we promptly received a "cease and desist" letter from none other than the makers of Cheers!

I'm not quite sure who spotted our commercial and turned us in. We never learned their name, but they sure knew ours! And so my short-lived run on TV was over. At least, until we filmed another, less controversial commercial!

I Dream of Jeannie!

Speaking of television, no book on Bernard's Surf, let alone Cocoa Beach, would be complete without talking about the show that, in addition to the space program, put Cocoa Beach on the (national) map.

After all, a line in the TV show's opening jingle proclaimed how Jeannie followed the show's hero, Capt. Tony Nelson "… back to Cocoa Beach, a mythical town in a mythical state called Florida." [**Source:** *USA Today*] Not to mention occasional references to Cocoa Beach in the show and, once or twice (or so I've heard), even mention of the Surf itself.

Some might wonder why Cocoa Beach played so prominently in the show when, after all, most astronauts lived and trained in Houston, Texas, not our fair little beach town on the breezy east coast of Florida.

Well, I think I may know why: Sidney Sheldon was the producer/ director of *I Dream of Jeannie*. It just so happened that his uncle lived in Cocoa Beach. What's more, Sheldon's uncle used to come into the Surf all the time.

Well, lo and behold one day Sidney Sheldon walked into the lounge and introduced himself. Then he mentioned how he was producing this new show, *I Dream of Jeannie*, and would it be all right if, from time to time, they might mention the Surf in the show.

I told him I was flattered but had to admit that I hadn't seen the show since it played during prime time and, after all, I worked nights. He laughed and said that wouldn't be a problem.

When I did finally catch up to the show – in reruns, no less – I thought it was pretty funny how "Cocoa Beach, Florida" was portrayed as clearly Hollywood, California, since there's not a hill to be seen here in town for miles and miles, if any!

Still, it was flattering, even though I think the only thing they ever filmed here, if I recall correctly, was a "fake" wedding between stars Barbara Eden and Larry Hagman, which took place at Patrick Air Force Base.

It was more of a publicity stunt than anything, as I recall, but with the stars in town I figured it would be a prime opportunity to return Sidney Sheldon's favor of asking to use the restaurant in the show by inviting him and the cast to dinner.

Fortunately, they accepted and we were proud to host Mr. Sheldon and his wife, as well as series stars Larry Hagman, Barbara Eden and her husband, Michael Ansara, for dinner.

I wish I had pictures to share with you, with everybody, from this historic meeting but you know, I was always very protective of my guests' privacy. I just felt like if I had invited them to dinner, it would be rude of me to then ask them to spend half their time posing for pictures. Little did I know, they probably would have liked that more than the dessert!

Years later in 1973, on a trip to Los Angeles to watch the Miami Dolphins play in the Superbowl, we were fortunate enough to dine with the gracious Bill Daily at his home in LA. For you TV buffs, you might recall that Daily played the affable Major Healy on *I Dream of Jeannie* and was kind enough to invite us to his home for dinner.

Howdy, Neighbor

I first met Martin Caidin at the old Phoenix restaurant in Cape Canaveral, which is odd considering he lived right across the street from me on Bayshore Drive at the time.

Caidin was the author of numerous popular books including *Marooned, Samurai* and *Black Thursday*, but is most famous for writing the novel *Cyborg*, on which the TV show *The Six Million Dollar Man* and its spinoff series, *The Bionic Woman*, were both based.

Caidin was also an expert on aeronautics and aviation and to get him to talk about flying was a little like getting me to talk about FSU football. In other words, good luck getting him to stop!

Chapter 12:

A Changing of the Guard

In every restaurant, there is an ebb and flow, a tide of sorts that goes in and out depending on the season, the year and what is going on in the lives of its management and employees.

The Surf was no different. In fact, if there *has* been one constant in my life as a restaurant owner it's been the inevitability of turnover. Sometimes it's one of your favorite waitresses or hostesses quitting, other times it's as simple as watching one of your strongest summer season busboys or bar backs head back to college in the fall, leaving you to find his replacement – which often takes two or more employees to fill his hardworking shoes.

But other times the employee is a little harder to replace than with somebody's cousin or brother or a Classified ad in *Florida Today*. And sometimes, that employee can be near impossible to replace:

Bittersweet Opportunity: *The Legend of Charlie Rags*

One day in the early 90s, Charlie Ragland came into my office just like any other day, but it turns out this *wasn't* any other day after all. Sitting down across from my desk, he lit right in. "Rusty," he said, perhaps before he could chicken out. "I have an opportunity and I think it's too good to pass up…"

When I asked him what kind of an opportunity, he proceeded to tell me that he had the chance to partner in a new restaurant opening in Houston, Texas.

I don't mind telling you, my heart kind of did a double beat that day. Houston just seemed so far away, and I could tell by the excitement in Charlie's voice that he had already kind of made up his mind about taking the job. Still, he was the kind of guy who wanted me to know how he felt about the decision, even if it *was* a foregone conclusion.

I asked him what he thought about it and he said it was a once in a lifetime thing, the kind of opportunity he just couldn't pass up. "I think this is my chance to do something for myself," is how I remember him putting it, and having taken that kind of chance myself by taking over the family business years earlier, I knew just what he was talking about.

At the same time, and perhaps selfishly, I couldn't help but think how losing Charlie to his own outfit would affect our organization. While there had certainly been days before Charlie, and would clearly be days after – especially since he seemed so dead set on leaving – he had been there for most of my restaurant education and through most of the Surf's ups and downs to that point.

His knowledge of the back of the house, the numbers he needed to meet and how much of this to order and how much of that, were nothing short of rocket science as far as I was concerned. Replacing him wouldn't be easy, but it was the last thing on my mind as I shook his hand.

"So," he prodded, "what do you think I should do?"

"Go for it," I told him. And that was that. It was not as casual a response as it sounded but, instead, a ringing endorsement. I already knew he was going to do it anyway, so why cloud his decision with doubts or regrets? Sink or swim, I knew Charlie had to do what Charlie had to do, and only he could make the final decision about his own future.

He seemed equal parts surprised and relieved by *my* enthusiasm for *his* enthusiasm. But I knew, from experience, he was going to need as much luck as he could get from everyone who knew him well before he headed off to meet an uncertain fate.

Taking over an existing restaurant, one with an established clientele and a solid brand and reputation, wasn't easy. Starting one from scratch was doubly difficult. I knew Charlie had some tough days ahead of him, and I think he did, too, but we both knew it was the kind of thing he had to try and do for himself. Otherwise he'd just have that regret hanging over his head the entire time he stayed at the Surf, wondering about what "could have been."

And knowing Charlie like I do, I think if I had pulled some drama, if I had given him some line about how "invaluable" he was, and how hard he'd be to replace, he might have even bought into it and stuck around, just out of blind loyalty. But showing up to work and actually being there are two very different things, and I didn't want Charlie to stick around one place when he'd rather be somewhere else entirely.

And it wasn't like I'd never had thoughts of leaving myself. As fond as I was of the Surf, its staff and its customers, there's a time, I think, in every man's life where he looks at where he is and wonders where he might like to be instead.

In college I'd been working toward becoming a high school PE teacher, with my eye on coaching the sport I'd grown up playing and had actually gotten a scholarship to play at FSU: football.

Lou's offer to work for the Surf during my junior year of college had put that particular life plan on hold, while Bernard's death had put those dreams on ice – seemingly permanently. I often wondered how my life might be different if I'd said "no" to my father and gone back to FSU, or if Bernard had lived and gotten better and come back to the restaurant full-time.

Where would I be then?

What would I be doing?

How different might my life be?

Seeing Charlie chomping at the bit to head off into uncharted territories and make a path for himself way off in Texas just reminded me of how big the world was beyond my own little corner of Minuteman Causeway and A1A.

But as often as I had those thoughts, the reality was that the Surf was my home and losing Charlie meant I had to redouble my efforts to make sure the Surf survived, even thrived, in Charlie's absence.

I'm not going to lie; it wasn't easy! I'd predicted replacing Charlie would be a tall order and, man, was it ever. I'd say we went through three or four managers in the two years Charlie was gone. No offense to them if they're reading this, but it takes a special breed to run a place like the Surf, and while I was happy to fill in while they were getting their feet wet I wasn't going to start pulling double duty this late in the game, either.

I expected any General Manager, Charlie or otherwise, to act like one and when they didn't, or couldn't, it was time to look for somebody who could. Somehow we limped along, and probably would have kept limping along if Charlie hadn't come back to visit some family in the area and asked if we could have dinner while he was in town.

I was eager to hear how he was making out in Texas and jumped at the chance, only to learn a few minutes into the meal that things hadn't gone quite as well out in Houston as Charlie had hoped.

His restaurant, Charlie Rag's, had shuttered and Charlie wasn't just back in the area visiting family, he was actively looking for work. (Little did I know at the time he was being courted by my best friend Larry Garrison and Cape Canaveral Hospital!) Over the course of that meal, by hook or by crook, I hired Charlie back.

Just like that, the team was back together again. But I knew it hadn't been easy for Charlie to admit he'd failed, just as I knew it wouldn't be easy for him to go back to being GM after having his own place, let alone one with his own name on it!

But the fact is I respected Charlie for what he'd gone and tried to do, and I for one knew that his restaurant's failure wasn't for his lack of trying. If Charlie's one thing he's a workaholic, and I knew if he'd worked his tail off for me, he'd worked twice as hard to make a go of his own place.

I can't say I didn't see it coming. I don't mean to sound like Nostradamus, but there's a reason the majority of new restaurants that open fail: it's because it's damn hard work to get people to try something new and unproven when there is already so much old and proven out on the market for them to choose from.

Particularly in this day and age of chain restaurants and big names and a franchise on every corner, to try and start something new, of your own, without a "Fridays" or "Donalds" or "Garden" or "Lobster" as your last name, is extremely difficult. And to succeed within a year or two, without the funding, patience or resources to last a good four or five years before people start to know and trust you, well, that may be the hardest part of all.

But I also knew it had to be done, one way or another. For better or worse, Charlie had to go and do it, and whatever he may say about it now, and we've talked about it a couple of times since those days, the fact is he probably wouldn't have done it any other way.

Would he have rather succeeded? Obviously, and I'd be far happier writing a different ending to this story by telling you to go and visit Charlie at his thriving restaurant out in Houston! But failure isn't an ending, anyway. From Across the Street to Charlie Rag's, everything that doesn't kill a restaurateur just makes him that much hungrier.

Hungrier for success, that is.

And because of that experience, I also knew that when Charlie came back to the Surf, he'd see things a little differently than he may have before. It's one thing running a restaurant; it's another thing entirely to own one. I knew whatever choices he made from that moment on would be with that new perspective in mind, and I had no doubt Charlie would be back to his old pace in no time; and a few weeks later, he was.

I was happy to have Charlie back, but not happy about why he'd come back. As many managers as we'd gone through while he was away, I would have kept going through them until I found a worthy replacement, and happily so, if it meant Charlie was off running a successful place of his own there in Houston.

Me Rusty, You Jane

One thing I'll always be grateful to Charlie for, in addition to his years of loyal service and friendship over the years, is the fact that he talked me into hiring my longtime assistant, PR whiz and ultimately good friend, Jane Vester.

Jane had opened the Raw Bar at the Surf, one of its first and hardest working waitresses. She was loyal, dependable, quick and, above all, smart. In addition to working at the Raw Bar she was taking a full load at the University of Central Florida and, when she graduated with a degree in Marketing, she wasn't quite sure what she wanted to do with it.

Charlie saw her wavering between a few opportunities and knew we needed to snatch her up before somebody else took her off the job market. It just so happened I was in the market for a new assistant after my old one left.

Charlie came into my office one day and said, "Rusty, I'm telling you, you need to hire this girl before somebody else does. She's just the right thing for you."

Charlie was usually pretty good about judging people and hell, I thought, if Jane worked half as hard in the office as she did in the Raw Bar, how could I miss?

I wasn't sure Jane would go for it, since she'd put so much time and effort into getting her degree, but I think she saw my job offer as a good opportunity to stay close to home, with an organization she already knew and trusted, and a way to use her skills and still have plenty of time with her growing family.

Well, Charlie was right. Not only did Jane hop right into the office job with both feet and all hands on deck, but she went above and beyond the call at every opportunity. I say "assistant" but that's not the right word for what Jane was... to me, for me, or to and for the Surf organization.

It wasn't long before Jane quickly put her marketing degree to work in ways both big and small. Whether it was the ad copy for the two-for-one dinner specials in the back of the "TGIF" section of *Florida Today* or convincing me to do more radio spots or simply using her connections in the community to come up with fun events, Jane excelled at building the Surf brand. She was also a detail person, and as a result made the office twice as efficient in half the time.

The same way Jane had done double duty when she worked in the Raw Bar and attended UCF, I always felt she did two jobs over in the office: her regular office duties and marketing plus events.

Events were a big thing for Jane and she taught me to appreciate how valuable they could be in both spreading the brand and reaching out to the community. She always made a big deal out of the anniversary parties each October, and in that way she channeled my uncle Bernard to some degree.

She spearheaded many of the anniversary gifts we gave during her fifteen-year tenure with the Surf, from ashtrays to rocks glasses to wine glasses and how many to order and how to hand them out in an orderly fashion. In fact, if you attended one of our anniversary parties in the 80s or 90s and had a good time, you can thank Jane!

But it wasn't just special events or anniversaries where Jane excelled; her devotion to all things Bernard's Surf lasted all year long. From remembering which astronaut liked which wine to coordinating the events surrounding John Glenn's return into space after three decades, Jane was on top of it… and then some.

The funny thing was, and I don't think either of them would dispute this, Jane and Charlie fought like cats and dogs! I doubt any customers knew, or most of the employees, but those two… phew! I just find it so ironic because Charlie was the first to suggest hiring her, and never would have considered firing her no matter how much grief she gave him, or vice versa.

He knew she was the best choice for the job, and how valuable she was to the organization. And whether she ever knew Charlie suggested her for the job or not, Jane respected him… but they argued about everything. I mean, everything!

From the design of the souvenir glasses to the food costs to the advertising budget to event menus, you had to admire their passion. Respect for each other? They both had it in spades. But you couldn't always tell it when the fur was flying in the office and I had to shut the door over to hear myself think!

The best part about those two was that, when the dust had settled and the wounds were bandaged, that was that. Back to business, get to work, and whatever decision had been made, they got it done, no questions asked.

I'll never forget the time we were sitting in Charlie's office and, mid-conversation, his head slumped forward. This was back when Charlie first started having problems with his heart and, thanks to a pacemaker they all got cleared up, but back in the day, man, it sure was touch and go there for awhile.

So there we were, I can't even remember what we were talking about at the time, but all of a sudden… Charlie slumps in his chair, passed out, dead to the world.

I was frozen, not sure what to do but Jane, tiny as she is, sprang into action. Without hesitating, she propped his head back, yanked open his mouth and started giving Charlie mouth to mouth resuscitation.

We're talking, full on the lips, frantically trying to bring her arch nemesis back to life! Sure enough, after a few huffs and puffs Charlie revived, looking at both of us like we were crazy! But that's how they were. Passions ran high, but their friendship ran deeper.

For me, the mark of a true professional isn't always acting like one when emotions flare, but putting those differences aside and getting the job done at the end of the day. And whatever words were said then, or how they might feel about it now, Charlie and Jane always got the job done.

And for that, I'm eternally grateful...

Chapter 13:

The More Things Change...

Imagine, if you will, a very different Cocoa Beach from the one that exists today. It will be easier for some than others, depending on how long you've lived here or how often you've visited our coastal town over the years. Imagine turning left from Minuteman Causeway onto A1A and cruising down the road, admiring the scenery as you travel north through our sunny little seaside town.

Pay particular attention to the restaurants that, once upon a time, lined both sides of A1A for pretty much as far as the eye could see. On the left you could just see Alma's and, in the little shopping center across from that, you'd find Pedro's.

On the right you could see the tropical oasis, complete with waterfall, that was Islander's Beef and Grog. Keep going and you'd see Krystal's burgers on the left, in front of the shopping center that once housed the TG & Y department store and A & P grocers, two of the few chains on the beach back then.

Keep going and you're getting into real prime territory. You've got the Ramada Inn and, right next door to that, the Holiday Inn, both popular with locals and tourists alike at the time. Even the astronauts could be found at these neighboring resorts. Photographer Ralph Morse captured a playful Deke Slayton diving into the Holiday Inn pool, in shirtsleeves and slacks, no less, for *LIFE* magazine in 1961.

Keep driving still and you'll find one of the town's other only chains, Burger Chef, and just past it G'Kedis restaurant. A little surf shop named Ron Jon's sits in a small strip mall that used to hold a florist, selling baggies and surf wax and, of course, surfboards.

Sit at the intersection of 520 and A1A and you have a couple of choices. Turn left and you'll find the locally famous and much-loved Ramon's and, just beyond that, the site of every post-sports game team dinner back in the day, Shakey's Pizzeria and, a little farther still you'll hit the Black Angus steakhouse and Gatsby's Sports Emporium. (I might be mixing up my eras here a little bit, but… you get the general idea!)

Keep going straight up A1A toward the Port and you'll find the Hong Kong house, owned by the Dong brothers, Harry and Larry. Just past that you'd find the Mouse Trap, a local legend and, farther along, just before you get to the port which is pretty much where civilization ended on the beach back in the day, you'd find the Moon Hut, a tiny little diner style eatery with a fiberglass "moon" face over the front door.

Now, wake up, snap your fingers, open your eyes and you're back in 2021! They're all gone, every last one of them. From the Beef and Grog to Alma's, from Desperados to Burger Chef and Shakey's and Ramon's and G'Kedis, all gone.

Only Ron Jon's remains on the strip, same as it ever was, though not really since it takes up an entire block now and glows, neon pink, blue and green 24-hours a day, 365-days a year. It's our very own Disney World and, gradually over time, the rest of A1A has tried valiantly to duplicate that type of big-name brand and, quite frequently, neon color scheme.

New restaurants and lounges have come (and, in some cases, quickly gone) to take the place of the old. The old Alma's is now Slow 'n Low, the old Shakey's became Italian Courtyard became Long Doggers. The old Black Angus is Florida Seafood now and the old Gatsby's is Sunset Bar & Grille. The Mousetrap has been a few things since it closed, most of them steakhouses. The Cocoa Beach Fish Camp Grill sits there now.

I doubt many folks who go in for a cold beer and a lap dance realize it, but the new Cheaters is the old Hong Kong house, once the finest – and only – sit down Chinese restaurant on the beach.

I suppose every town could tell the same story: businesses open and close nearly every day, and there but for the grace of God went I for nearly 50 years. And I'm not immune. After all, Bernard's Surf is no more – and how that happened is a story I'll get to shortly.

But I suppose my point is that if my three other uncles had tried to dissuade Bernard from opening a restaurant back in 1948 when the slate was clean and the Cocoa Beach horizon was unbroken, how hard do you think it is to open one today, when everyone and their brother wants the same meal, prepared the same way, at the same price, as every other chain restaurant in the country?

And when I say, "There but for the grace of God go I," I mean it. Many, many times the Surf was on rocky ground over the years, and if it wasn't for a bank loan here or a cash infusion from my old man there, we would have joined those other big names in Cocoa Beach's "restaurant graveyard" far sooner than we ultimately did.

But we were always fortunate enough to find someone who believed in us just enough to keep us afloat. I'll never forget sometime in the late 80s or early 90s, after yet another national recession that trickled down to the local level, we were on the ropes again. I can't remember the exact figure but I believe our net profit, after all was said and done for the year, was $25,000… give or take.

Not for a month, but for the entire year. To stay afloat, I had to go to the bank and ask for a loan. And they weren't going to give it to me. One of the loan officers at the time, Shari Evetts, worked hard to get the loan approved. (As she would go on to do many other times throughout the years!) But, unfortunately, it wasn't Shari's call.

Folks above her had to approve the loan, and they weren't having it. Can you believe it? As long as we'd been in business, all the fees we'd paid over the years, and the loan committee considered us a "bad bet."

Fortunately, Dr. Joe Von Thron was on the Board of Directors and when he heard how dire the situation was, he stepped in. "Look," he must have told the committee in one way or another, "this family has been in business for nearly 50 years. They practically founded Cocoa Beach, and if Rusty's taken a beating this year, I know he's asking for a fair amount and he'll use it to come out on top next year…"

Sure enough, they listened to Joe… and gave us the loan. And sure enough, Joe was right; we *did* come back, better than ever. But we couldn't have if it wasn't for that quick cash infusion at just the right time.

How many restaurants, I wonder, didn't get the same chance as I did, right when I needed it the most? How many restaurants didn't have a loan officer or board member going to bat for them just when they needed that little push to get them over the hump? It's the little things like that, the personal touch and the professional connections of a small town that have always made me love Cocoa Beach, even when the road was rocky and the future uncertain.

I can remember another time I was up for yet another loan – I told you we were on the ropes a lot! – and I was so blind I couldn't even read the documents I was signing. Literally.

I'd gone to a funeral out of town and, in a hurry, had packed the wrong contact lens container. When I went to put them in the next morning I knew right away something was wrong, but I was out of town and the funeral was about to start and I had no choice but to keep them in so I could see what I was doing.

They started stinging almost right away, and it got worse and worse as the day went on. By the time I got back home to Cocoa Beach, I could hardly open my eyes. My then wife Sherrell took me to the emergency room and apparently I'd grabbed an old container and the contacts had cracked, scratching my retina.

The doctor said I'd recover, but it could take up to a week before I was seeing normally again. Until then, I'd be virtually blind. Well, it just so happened I had to meet with the loan officer that very week.

Fortunately he let me come to his house and discuss the loan there since I might have destroyed his office down at the bank! Sherrell drove me there and guided me to the door, but after that I was on my own.

The loan officer helped me to a seat, walked me through some questions, I gave him the best answers I could but, between you and me, the only reason I think I got that loan was out of sympathy!

Either way, I'll take it any way I can get it!

My Own Personal Declaration of Independence

For years my kids wondered why I would always choose a Mom and Pop restaurant over a glitzy national chain whenever we went on vacation, even if it was a little shady and the service wasn't so hot. I think now they know that if we don't at least try and give our business to the independent restaurants when we can, America as we know it will die off, as it appears to be doing today.

And it's not just restaurants. The other day I was talking to Rusty Jr. and he was mentioning how wouldn't it be nice if somebody "did something" with downtown Cocoa Beach.

"Like what?" I asked.

"You know," he said, somewhat innocently, "cleaned it up, made everything nice and neat like at Downtown Disney or the Avenues down in Viera."

I think he knew what he was saying before he finished saying it, but I cut him off and reminded him of the many fine and independent businesses doing great things downtown. From our favorite sushi restaurant to Juice 'N Java to Heidi's Jazz Club and beyond, to the Fat Donkey and the Tiny Turtle, I'm proud to say that Cocoa Beach has always fought to keep its independent spirit and open arms to new businesses wanting to make a go of it. The more eclectic, the better.

I like to think that, in many ways, it's the same pioneer spirit that met Uncle Bernard when he first wanted to open the Surf back in 1948, even as his three brothers tried to talk him out of it.

Don't get me wrong. I enjoy a good, quality chain restaurant as much as the next guy, especially the newer trend of upscale eateries that rival some of the independents in quality and style, say a Bonefish Grille or even Carrabbas.

I also know that they employ many fine people the same way the Surf did all those years, and Alma's and Pedro's and Shakey's and the Mouse Trap years before that.

But if everybody would just try one independent, Mom 'N Pop restaurant for every Outback, Carrabba's or Subway they visit, it's my firm belief that this country would be better off, and many more businesses would stay in business rather than join that ugly "restaurant graveyard" I keep talking about.

And it's not just restaurants, but every independent business. Cocoa Beach is a small town, and I've been fortunate enough to work alongside great friends and neighbors at 2 South Atlantic Avenue over the years.

Again, a lot of the businesses that used to border the Surf are no longer there anymore. From record stores to gift shops to shell shops to souvenir stands to pizza parlors to game rooms, the landscape at the intersection of Minuteman and A1A – which has been my home away from home for more years than I can count – has changed, much as the rest of the country has changed.

There was B & K Records just a few doors down from the Surf, where my son Rusty Jr. bought his first album ever. (Something by someone called "Meatloaf," if I recall correctly!) There was Frank's Seaside Pizza across the street, once owned by my former General Manager at Rusty's at the Port, Frank Stevens. And, of course, for as many years as I can remember, there was Ann Lia's gift shop. Run by Paul Godke, Ann Lia's was the kind of gift shop-slash-stationary store you just don't see any more.

It had a little bit of everything, and something for everyone: greeting cards, figurines, household goods, toys, games, puzzles, calendars, you name it, Paul had it. I can't tell you how many times I remembered an anniversary, birthday or holiday at the last minute – or, to be honest, someone in the office remembered one for me! – and I was able to walk one door down to Ann Lia's and find exactly what I needed.

With a little help from Paul, of course.

My sons were just the same. Most of my good friends, colleagues, family and, of course, business neighbors had house accounts at the Surf, and more often than not they returned the favor by offering me an account at their places of business as well. Ann Lia's was no exception.

How many gifts Rusty Jr. bought his brother Rhett on my Ann Lia account, and Rhett bought Rusty, I lost track of over the years. Of course, Paul didn't have the greatest selection if you were a teenage boy, and I think the annual tradition of Rhett buying his older brother birthday presents at Ann Lia's stopped when he gave Rusty Jr. a cat calendar… for his sixteenth birthday.

Still, more years than I care to count there were Ann Lia's gifts under the tree and wrapped as Christmas presents for my (mostly) unsuspecting family. Then again, they probably knew Ana-Lia's inventory as well as I did, so I wasn't really fooling anybody. Which made it all the sadder when, a few years back, poor Paul had a heart attack while manning the counter at his store one day.

I was there, waiting for the ambulance with his wife when he passed away, and there at his funeral a few days later when friends old and new, and customers alike, showed up to pay their respects to a local legend who, year after year, sold us all greeting cards and last-minute gifts. In a way, Paul's passing – and the shuttering of Ann Lia's gift shop to make way for something new – helped mark the end of an era.

Chapter 14:

Happy Anniversary, Bernard

Bernard's Surf first opened its doors on October 31, 1948, and every year since, from Bernard's era to mine, we have always celebrated the event with a big party in honor of not just Bernard and his vision for the Surf, but for our loyal customers as well.

As with most things that continued his lasting legacy, it all started with Bernard wanting to mark the occasion in his own inimitable style. He was a stylish man with big dreams and, for him, these anniversaries were a chance to mark how far he'd come and to thank those who'd helped him achieve another year's worth of goals.

Back in the late 40s and early 50s, of course, style was a very different thing, and Bernard fit that era to a "T" with his fancy suits, wide ties and wider smile. He loved to entertain his friends, old and new, and was better at it than most. People loved him for it, and year after year not only did the Surf grow in success and popularity, but so did his Halloween anniversary parties.

Once upon a time we celebrated with hundreds of pounds of steamed shrimp, free for the taking, as a "thank you" to our loyal customers for coming in all year long. Year after year, word spread about the suckers giving out "free shrimp" down in Cocoa Beach and folks we'd never seen before showed up to chow down on their fill.

The last time we ever gave away free shrimp, Dad gave me 1,000-pounds from his seafood "fleet" and I bought another 1,000-pounds from local distributors. That's a lot of shrimp, and I knew we'd give away every last one. That's because as early as April, we'd start getting phone calls: "Are you still having your anniversary party in October?"

"Yes, ma'am."

"And will you still be giving away all the free shrimp you can eat?"

"Yes, ma'am."

"Oh, great. And, one more question... how do I get there again?"

With each new call, it became clear that it wasn't the regular customers we were cooking all that shrimp for, but folks who just wanted a free meal one night out of the year.

That last year we gave out over 2,000-pounds of shrimp and I believe half of them walked out of the restaurant stuffed in women's purses and men's jacket pockets! That was when we realized we needed to put a stop to the madness, so we shifted gears and switched to something a little more permanent for our anniversary giveaway.

That's when the era of gifts began. Bernard was a big gift giver, always having a secret stash of Surf memorabilia to give out to his favorite, best or most frequent customers. From engraved lighters to letter openers to cuff links, Bernard personified that "Mad Men" era of old school class, charm and, above all, attention to detail.

He loved to give out birthday presents, and was always handing out these very stylish, very elaborate gifts to patrons and even employees on birthdays, anniversaries and over the holiday season.

There was a company at the time that specialized in engraved gifts and I believe they'd wait to send their salesman over to the Surf when they knew Bernard was having a cocktail or two at the end of another long shift and show him their new line of lighters, pill boxes or cigarette cases.

Sure enough, Bernard would order a few hundred or so, tell them to slap the Surf logo on it and that's what folks would get for their birthdays for the next two years or so. At least, that is, until the supplies ran out and they sent over a new salesman to sell Bernard the latest thing in personalized giveaways.

He had style, he had class and, above all, he was exceedingly generous. Over the years, I tried my hardest to learn from his example. Keeping up the anniversary tradition was definitely one of Bernard's legacies I wanted to continue, and continue it I did.

I wasn't as big a gift giver as Bernard, and I tried not to fall for savvy salesmen when they showed up during my shift drink, but I believed Bernard was on the right track by making generosity, style and class a big part of the Surf brand.

For years we made the little touches a big deal at the Surf, with monogrammed matchbooks, drink stirrers and even little black doilies that went on top of the saucer and under a fresh cup of coffee, all bearing the trademark Bernard's Surf logo.

Even as times changed and we gradually did away with more and more of those little touches, mostly due to the continually rising prices of such "extras," I always insisted on cocktail napkins. Crisp and white, Bernard's Surf in black on top, whenever I tended bar, whoever tended bar, I wanted a cocktail napkin under every drink.

It was a little thing, I know, but whether it was an everyday regular or a brand-new patron, I wanted them to know that we stood for quality, class and style.

And frankly, I believe, people noticed that kind of thing. Maybe not consciously, but subconsciously, in the back of their minds. If you didn't use a cocktail napkin one time, then skipped it another time, they'd notice. And maybe they'd think, "Hmm, where'd that go? They're not doing that anymore? Maybe they're cutting back on cocktail napkins. Well, what else are they cutting back on?"

And that's how a brand erodes, I believe. That's how customer loyalty fades away, and that's how you lose a customer here, and a customer there, so if I gave you a cocktail napkin even when you didn't want one, well, now you know why. (And thanks for coming back!)

A Holiday Tradition

I never got the chance to ask Bernard if he purposefully chose Halloween to open the Surf for any nostalgic or personal reason, or if it was simply the day his liquor permit got approved or the beer cooler finally got put in.

Personally, we tended to mark the actual Surf anniversary privately, as a family, and then began opening up the 31st as a way to publicly thank folks for being loyal customers all year long. Either way, people sure loved to come and celebrate two occasions at once: Halloween and the Surf's anniversary.

It was great for us, too, because we got to let our hair down and come in costume as well. Now, anyone can tell you I'm not a big costume person, but I've been known to get in the holiday spirit and show up as a pirate or a bandito, or one time even a woman in a tennis dress.

But the servers and, in particular, the customers put me to shame.

Over the years I've forgotten more costumes than I can remember, but those that stick out include, let me see... some guy dressed like a Budweiser beer can, or Mark Shroble, who came dressed as a box of Bernard's Surf matches one year.

Thanks to Juli Shroble some of the server's more fantastic costumes are forever recorded for posterity, including Raggedy Ann, Lady Liberty, a playing card, a pumpkin, a princess and even a life-size dollar bill.

When I think of how long the Surf lasted, and how many costume contests were won and lost over the years, it truly boggles the mind. The holiday was special for the Fischer family, to be sure, but I hope that over the years Halloween meant as much to my customers as well, whether they dressed up or not.

With Our Compliments...

Of course, the other tradition I borrowed from Bernard was the gifts he gave out every year. I couldn't exactly afford to give out engraved lighters to hundreds of guests each Halloween, so we settled on anniversary glasses: one per guest, come one, come all, first come, first serve, as long as they lasted.

Rocks glasses. Tumblers. Juice glasses. Coffee cups and, okay, the occasional ashtray or shot glass. Each souvenir featured the original Surf logo first designed by Bernard, depicting an old shrimp boat with its nets out, and the original Surf slogan: "From our fishing fleet to you." And the date, of course, as well as the year we were celebrating.

Fifty plus years of souvenirs and I have at least one of each in storage somewhere, give or take. Counting them down you can see the glass styles change over the years, from the frosted white of a 1950s coffee mug to the old-style champagne flute from the 60s.

But year after year, people came to expect them and, despite the expense of ordering 500+ glasses every anniversary, I was glad to see old friends and new alike walk out of the restaurant clutching their anniversary gift.

I'm sure that, somewhere out there, there are folks who probably have almost as many glasses in their collection as I do. Couples who came in, year after year, regulars who had probably been there at the very first grand opening and wanted a nice, quiet "anniversary" dinner in the early evening hours before the madness of the costume parties and Halloween drink specials began as the night wore on.

I always thought it was great that so many generations came to celebrate the Surf's anniversary for so many different reasons. Whether it was to try and win a $20 gift certificate in the costume or pumpkin carving contest, to get a free rocks glass with the Surf logo on it or simply to watch the waitresses rush around in their sexy French maid or I Dream of Genie costumes, I was happy to give the grownups in town a great place to celebrate Halloween after all the little trick-or-treaters were home in bed, sleeping off their candy dreams.

Of course, there are always hiccups as the years stack up. I'll never forget the year we added wrong and celebrated our 29th anniversary, on the Surf's 28th year in business! While it was too late to recall the glasses by the time someone with a sharper eye than myself noticed, all we could do was wait until next year… and celebrate the Surf's 29th anniversary all over again!

Roller Boogie!

I can sit here now and fondly recall those evenings, but at the time they were hectic affairs that were always one crashing tray or irate customer away from complete and utter disaster.

Just like the spillover crowds that greeted Bernard's original grand opening back in 1948, every year the crowds grew and grew. I can remember one of my first years after taking over from Bernard, the bar was so busy one of our cocktail waitresses put on roller skates to make sure she got her orders to their tables on time!

She'd order her drinks at the old, straight bar we used to have in the 60s, head out the bar door that opened out toward the intersection of Minuteman and A1A, roller skate south down the sidewalk parallel with A1A and go in the dining room door off the street side to deliver her drinks to the dining patrons inside. Then back out the door and up the street when she got another new order!

Things got a little bit easier for the servers after we remodeled the entire lounge in the 70s, but it was never quite "easy," no matter how much room we had. Which, as they say in the restaurant business, is what we call a good problem to have!

Chapter 15:

Challenged

1985 brought good news and bad for The Surf. In the bad news department, my good friend and mentor Bob Moore decided to retire from running the package store. He was the driving force behind the package store's success for decades and, frankly, I wasn't interested in finding anyone to replace him.

What was the good news? Charlie Ragland was back. After taking a few years off to try his hand at running a restaurant in his home state of Texas, Charlie came back ready to throw himself into The Surf with new vitality, energy and ideas. The timing couldn't have been better, even if business was in the pits.

With a few thousand feet of space just sitting there without a manager to run it, Charlie and I decided to close the package store and re-open a new section of the restaurant in its place. ABC had opened just down the street and killed a good part of our liquor store business anyway, and we were looking to get out of retail and use that space for the restaurant instead.

The plan was for something called the Skylight Room. We built a makeshift stage in one corner and wanted to bring in live entertainment, try some different dishes, somewhere in between the full course meals of the Red Room and the more casual dining fare being offered by a wider array of chain restaurants opening up locally and in Merritt Island.

It was also a great, big space for banquets, catering and other special occasions. The sky was the limit, the possibilities were endless and the future looked bright.

What could possibly go wrong?!?

A Space Program in Peril

The "Skylight Room" experiment was an exciting one, but doomed to failure from the start. Partly it was a bad idea, partly it was bad timing. While the country was moving in the direction of more casual dining, with chain restaurants like Bennigan's, Applebee's and TGI Friday's opening up all over the country it seemed, we were moving in the opposite direction: hoping for private parties and long, slow, lingering dinners accompanied by classy, sedate live music.

It limped along for a few months, but shortly after closing the package store and opening the Skylight Room, disaster struck in the timing department. On January 28, 1986, the Space Shuttle Challenger exploded in the skies above the Space Coast.

It was both a personal and professional tragedy for just about everyone in Brevard. Much like we all remember where we were when President Kennedy was shot, so do those of us on the Space Coast remember where we were when the Challenger blew up. I was standing in the doorway of the Surf lounge, like so many of my patrons that day, looking up into the blue sky expecting another flawless NASA shuttle launch, when disaster struck instead.

I'll never forget the sick feeling in the pit of my stomach as I turned back to go inside and watch the news, hearing our worst fears confirmed as we sat there around the bar, in shock, at what we'd just witnessed with our very own eyes. Everyone who witnessed the launch that day knew what they'd seen, even if few of us could verbalize the grim reality of what we'd just witnessed: none of the seven brave astronauts on board could have possibly survived that deadly blast.

And, sadly, they hadn't...

This was back in the day when the shuttle program was still fairly new and, as a result, schools and businesses still let their students and employees out to watch each launch. Rusty Jr. remembers standing in front of Cocoa Beach High School, watching the launch when it burst into flames and left a scar of orange and smoke across the sky.

His fellow students were the sons and daughters of engineers, technicians and staff at NASA and already they knew what the future held, and it wasn't good. They weren't the only ones. I knew that tragedy for the space program also meant hard times for the Space Coast, and sooner rather than later.

The result was immediate and, I suppose, inevitable. In order to ensure the safety of the brave men and women of the shuttle program, the space program was essentially shut down for two years. Or, at least, launches were.

I can remember NASA doing essentially the same thing after the fire that claimed the lives of Gus Grissom and his crew in that deadly accident atop the Apollo rocket back in the 60s. As I remember it, the space program essentially went into hibernation for a year or so until they'd found the root of the problem and made sure it wouldn't happen again.

Back then, of course, the economy of Cocoa Beach and Cape Canaveral were just beginning to merge with that of the space program. By 1986, the two were inextricably linked and one could hardly survive without the other.

Not only did we depend on the tourists who flooded into the county to visit Kennedy Space Center and for weeks before, during and after launch days for our livelihoods, but NASA employees who lived in the area year round were our bread and butter.

It was a crippling blow to local businesses, but particularly restaurants and other "luxury" items that weren't necessarily essential to folks who might have lost their jobs, however temporarily. Don't forget most of the families on the Space Coast were involved in the program, either directly or indirectly.

Engineers, scientists, technicians, whatever, whoever, they all depended on the safety and security of the space program, and suddenly all of that was in jeopardy. No one was really in the mood for two-hour dinners or live entertainment anymore, let alone lavish catered affairs in a private room. Which, of course, was exactly what we'd designed the new Skylight Room for.

It wasn't exactly as if the Surf was on solid ground before the Challenger disaster, anyway. The country had already been through two mini-recessions and as a business we'd faced the fear of imminent bankruptcy more than once. The bank was calling every so often about late, or missing, mortgage checks. Somehow we'd managed to hang on, but who knew for how long now?

There's only so much you can cut in the restaurant business before you have to quit calling yourself a restaurant. Quality had always been Bernard's first priority and had always been #1 with me as well; quality staff, quality food, quality preparation, quality atmosphere, and the more you cut, the more you sacrifice quality for cost.

And you have to have a certain number of staff on hand. After all, Charlie and I could only bus so many tables, make so many drinks, expedite so many trays of food, before people started thinking "fire sale" and started going to some safe, stable, generic chain restaurant for their evening out instead.

Charlie clearly recalls the day he had to sit the entire staff down, everyone from managers to assistant managers, cooks to busboys, servers to the girls in the salad room and tell them that not only would we be cutting benefits and hours to save the business, but it might be a year or more until they all got them back.

He wanted to know, then and there, would the staff be up for doing more with less in the foreseeable future. He was giving them a choice, to stay or go, with the full knowledge that life as they knew it – to say nothing of the size of their weekly paychecks – was about to change drastically, as it already had for Charlie and me.

He only recalls one employee quitting that day. It was a testament, I believe, to how loyal the Surf's employees had always been over the years, and continue to be to this day.

It was a tough decision, and a hard question to ask, but as usual the dedicated staff and employees of the Surf rose to the occasion. Now it was our turn to make sure the sacrifices we were all making were worth it.

The only question remaining was… how the hell were we going to do that?

Tough Times and Tight Shorts: *The Birth of a Raw Bar*

Little did we know it, but inspiration was just around the corner, in the form of tight shorts, big screen TVs, cold pitchers of beer and hot chicken wings.

Getting desperate as business only got worse through 1986 and 1987, Charlie and I began taking "road trips" seeking inspiration for "the next big thing" to replace the dead on the vine Skylight Room with.

We traveled all through the South, up to Atlanta, Georgia, over to Tampa, down to Miami and back up to Orlando. We saw a lot of great ideas that, frankly, Charlie and I knew were going to be fads, or that wouldn't go over well in our neck of the woods, or that were simply out of our league to execute, expense wise. And after a long day of scouting out restaurants and food courts and trade shows, Charlie and I would always wind up at the same kind of restaurant that suited our style the most: one of the casual sports bars – Charlie and I started calling them "wing chains" – that had opened up all around the country in the mid- to late-80s.

You know the ones: a big screen TV blaring in every corner, butcher block tables and paper towel rolls and cozy faux leather booths, cheap buffalo wing and beer specials, often times with scantily clad ladies in tank tops and short shorts asking you for another cold beer with a wink and a smile and a nod and a nudge.

It wasn't just the scantily clad ladies that kept us coming back to the same few sports bar-slash-wing chain restaurants at the end of another long day of scouting out new business ventures.

Okay, okay, so it might have *started* with the scantily clad ladies and their bountiful, ehhr, assets, but more than that it was the relaxed, casual atmosphere of these bustling, popular chain restaurants. After a long, often disappointing day of idea scouting, Charlie and I just wanted a cold pitcher of beer, a few dozen Buffalo wings, a lot of paper towels and some nice "scenery" to look at.

Still, I figured it might just be a guy thing and didn't really give it much more thought until my wife and I went on vacation to Sanibel Island that summer with my old pal Dave Ross and his then wife, Jan.

How the four of us wound up in a bustling strip mall wing and beer serving, chain sports bar is anybody's guess. But as we sat there, surrounded by TV screens and paper towel rolls and scantily-clad waitresses, the charm and the vibe and, above all, the popularity was unmistakable.

These "wing chains" had obviously struck a nerve and were clearly the right idea at the right time for the right type of customer. "Our" type of customer, I couldn't help thinking as I watched the crowds come and go. The bar was often standing room only, the servers were hustling here and there, the wings were literally flying out of the kitchen and, above all, the cash registers were ringing off the hook.

And it dawned on me, sitting there that day, picturing the vast but empty space Charlie and I had envisioned as the Skylight Room, just waiting for the right idea to bring it to life. "Why don't we open a seafood sports bar?" It would be just the thing after a long hot day on the beach or out at the Space Center, sunburned tourists looking for a place to cool off and fuel up for their next adventure on the Space Coast. TVs blaring sports 24-7, groups of guys downing pitchers of beer while watching the big games all weekend, wing specials and raw oysters shucked right at the bar and, of course, scantily clad waitresses bustling back and forth.

It would be a great place for the locals to hang out during the off season as well. A casual atmosphere, cheap drink specials and happy hours, wings for just 25-cents each and plenty of paper towels, peel and eat shrimp with a bucket of beer, just the place to go after a long day surfing or, with later hours, a longer night working. And what's more, we could update and improve on an already successful business model with the quality service, seafood and, most importantly, menu that the fast growing "wing chains" lacked.

Bernard had built the Surf brand on a very simple philosophy: "From our fishing fleet to you." But it was more than just a brand spin or a catchy slogan. For those of us in Cocoa Beach and up and down the Space Coast, it was literally a way of life.

Many of our parents and grandparents had grown up in the "sleepy little fishing village" that had spawned our coastal community. We could honor that spirit by featuring fresh, local seafood along with wings and cold beer.

The four of us were getting excited, tossing out ideas, imagining possibilities and brainstorming all over the place. At one point I turned to the group and asked, "What would we call it?"

My wife thought for awhile, then snapped her fingers, eyes wide with inspiration. "Why not call it Rusty's?" she suggested. The rest of the group agreed.

I nodded, playing it cool, though secretly I was relieved someone else had suggested it! It would be a nice touch, frankly. For so long I'd run Bernard's Surf with my uncle's name on the sign. It would be nice to have my own name over the door – and on the staff's t-shirts – for a change!

It seemed a natural for the shot in the arm the business needed: casual, inexpensive fare, pitchers of beer, wings, oysters, steamed clams, fried shrimp baskets, the whole nine yards, all served by beautiful women in tight blue satin shorts!

The four of us returned home, hopped up on chicken wings and bright ideas. When I told Charlie about the idea, he loved it and, in true Charlie style, quickly sprung into action.

Always one to start with the high priority items first, he began by finding the perfect supplier for our first priority: skimpy blue shorts! And, to stand out from the rest of those national wing chains as much as possible, we decided on white and blue for our brand colors. They were casual, yet crisp and clean, almost nautical colors, a nice alternative to the more formal Red Room and even the more upscale Fischer's Lounge just up the stairs from where the Raw Bar would be located.

The only problem was, we were financially strapped and cash poor, and no bank was willing to lend us the money to turn the stodgy-by-comparison Skylight Room into the stripped down, modern, purposefully rustic looking Raw Bar.

So I went to Dad, hat in hand, and asked him for the money. I hated to do it, as he'd already been so good to me, financially speaking. But I felt it had to be done, and hopefully my old man would agree.

So there we sat, in Dad's penthouse apartment, me laying out my case, Lou and the rest of the family lobbing out objections and generally playing devil's advocate. It was far from easy, but after several blow ups and quite a few tears, begging and bartering, Lou lent me the $50,000 we needed to create the very first Rusty's Raw Bar.

By the time it opened in 1989, my estimation of its success was so far off the mark as to be almost comical if it wasn't so pitiful. I'd been so battered and bruised by the Challenger years, as I'd come to know them, and the lean years before that, that I thought we might do $200 to $300 in sales a day at the Raw Bar.

Charlie recalls the two of us standing next to each other on opening day, staring at the room we'd remodeled from scratch, a full staff of beautiful girls in short white tops and tight blue shorts, with no idea whether or not it would succeed.

"What do you need me to make a day for this to pay off?" Charlie asked that day, as Charlie was prone to do whenever we tried something new.

I shook my head. I quickly ran some figures in my mind, calculating what it might cost to make Dad's money back and pay off that $50,000 loan, sooner rather than later. I shrugged, resigned at this point merely to break even. "Do you think you can make $350 a day?"

Charlie nodded, as Charlie would. Whatever it took, Charlie was the Operations guy. He was going to make it happen, even if he had to go outside and yank passersby in off the street by their collars. "You got it," he said, though for once I had a hard time believing him.

But I should have. He did me a few times better than that, in fact: on opening day Rusty's Raw Bar made $1,000 and, fortunately, we never looked back. Each day, it seemed, we did better than the previous day.

In the first year alone, we did half a million dollars in oysters, wings, clam strips and pitchers of beer. It was an idea whose time had come, and thank God we took the chance or I might not be writing this book today. (Or, at least, not writing it in such a good mood!)

Timing is Everything

The success of Rusty's also changed the prospects for Bernard's Surf itself. The profits from Rusty's meant we could make some much needed changes to the rest of the restaurant as well, and we set about doing so almost immediately.

Part of the problem with the shrinking profits at the Surf wasn't just the Challenger disaster or the hard economic times, although they certainly contributed in a major way. But even without those challenges, the Surf would have been in trouble if we didn't take a long, hard look at where we'd been and focus on where we were going instead.

Tradition was one thing, but not when it got in the way of giving your customers what they wanted, in the here and now. The fact was, the way people were eating was changing. Not just in Cocoa Beach, but all over the country. The idea scouting trip Charlie and I had just taken hadn't just inspired Rusty's Raw Bar, but had changed our entire way of thinking about how people ate out nowadays.

It wasn't the 50s or 60s anymore, and we couldn't go on acting like it was. In the heyday of the Surf, people appreciated and savored the elaborate relish trays our kitchen staff labored over, heaped with celery and marinated peppers and apple rings (try finding those anymore!) and olives and relish for dipping, the fried mullet appetizers that came with every meal, the breadbasket heaped with sweet rolls and bread pudding and pumpernickel rolls and, of course, our famous onion board. But as times changed and tastes – and budgets – evolved to match, modern diners wanted cheaper, quicker, less lingering meals.

The days of cocktail hour and appetizers and coffee and dessert were far from over, but a new term, "casual dining," was truly starting to define how folks went out to eat in the 80s and beyond.

Sure, three- or four-course meals were fine for special occasions and family gatherings, but lots of folks just wanted a quick, inexpensive, tasty meal in casual surroundings. Particularly tourists, who we were depending on more and more for our annual income every year.

While it was important to cater to the locals, who were your bread and butter all year long, you couldn't do so if you weren't drawing in tourists during the busy seasons to help you stay in business while they were away and business in town had slowed to a crawl.

So the changes Charlie and I proposed were fairly far-reaching and would require taking some of the Raw Bar profits and funneling them into remodeling the rest of the Surf to fit the mood of the changing times.

While the Red Room continued to welcome long standing customers with finer taste buds and special occasions, we morphed the center of the restaurant into more casual dining fare, remodeling a circular bar as the center of the action and featuring smaller booths and tables for quicker, more casual dining and, not coincidentally, quicker turnover.

The Space Coast was evolving and, we hoped, so was the Surf:

Changing Times Requires a Changing Brand

Cocoa Beach is a strange, wonderful, eccentric place to live, let alone run a successful business. Most restaurants did one thing, and did it well. If you were a sushi bar, you drew a particular crowd and they knew what to expect when they walked through the door. Same with an Italian restaurant, a sports bar, a Mexican restaurant, a steak house, a barbecue rib joint or even a freestanding oyster bar.

As the 80s came and went and we found ourselves well into the early 90s, the Surf had gradually morphed into a hybrid of several restaurants under one roof. There was the Red Room in the back, which was as close as anyone was going to get to the original spirit of the Surf that Bernard envisioned when he opened the place way back in the 1940s.

Cocktails and rare steaks and leather booths and waiters and waitresses in traditional black and white attire, there for your service as long as you required. For a cost, that is. And, increasingly, it was a cost not all customers were prepared to pay.

Still, the Red Room was where you came when you wanted to impress a friend or out of town guest, close a business deal – as my friend Larry Garrison had decades earlier over margaritas and Doc Stahl's specials – or celebrate a birthday, anniversary, graduation or other special event.

Then you had Fischer's Lounge or, as my kids referred to it, the "adult bar" because that's where me and my friends and all our friends, the adults, hung out. It featured a simple lounge menu, full bar and a lively atmosphere that felt more like "Cheers" than the "Mad Men" throwback feel of the dark and brooding Red Room just beyond.

It was where you came if you were a regular, likely with your own seat at the bar – the same one every night. If you wanted to pop in for a quick bite after a game of golf or tennis at the Country Club, grab a late-night snack after a game of poker with the guys or enjoy a casual lunch over a cocktail or two, Fischer's Lounge had your number.

It was also where a lot of seniors came for a light, early dinner, so in addition to our lounge menu we offered an early bird menu featuring smaller meals for reasonable prices.

Downstairs was the original Rusty's Raw Bar, which attracted a younger crowed of tourists and locals alike, and continued to do gangbuster business that far exceeded any of our expectations.

Unlike the other two areas of the restaurant, which had shorter shelf lives and tended to do peak business during dinner hours, the Raw Bar typically had two to three fast, hot and standing room only rushes a day.

For instance, it was great for a quick lunch before or after a trip to the beach. However, it also held steady throughout the early afternoon and midday as business folks got off work or just wanted a cheap meal from the "happy hour" menu.

And after a usually steady dinner hour it continued doing well late into the night as other servers from competing restaurants came in for a shift drink and a dozen or two oysters, clams or wings before calling it a night. Or, in some cases, an early morning.

Occasionally Charlie and I would find ourselves amid another busy night and have to pinch ourselves, imaging how close we'd been to shuttering the Surf doors for good in the wake of the Challenger disaster.

Those employees who'd given up hours and even benefits during the lean times had gotten them back, and then some, and for me that was the most rewarding part of pulling ourselves back from the brink of financial disaster only a few short years before.

Professionally speaking, losing a business is obviously a disappointment but far from the end of the world. Personally, I'd worked with most of the Surf employees far too long to watch them lose their jobs, their livelihoods, if I could help it.

The success of Rusty's and some of the other changes we'd made in Fischer's Lounge and the Red Room meant that people could go on working, earning a paycheck and feeding their families.

And at the end of the day, for me anyway, that's what running a good restaurant is all about: feeding the families who come in for a meal and letting the employees who cook, serve and clean up after those meals go home and feed their families with a steady, and hopefully generous, paycheck as well.

How far we'd come from the package store that originally existed on the future site of Rusty's. To think that we'd almost called it quits as the poor Skylight Room sat empty, night after night. Now, with the Raw Bar booming and the original loan from Dad paid back in full, I could finally think about the future once more.

The Raw Bar concept was so popular we decided to open a second one at nearby Port Canaveral, a more logical location and a natural one for me since the Fischer name had been pivotal there since its very beginning.

We began construction on Rusty's Seafood & Oyster Bar at the Port in 1992 and finished by 1993, on the site where my brother Ronnie used to have his retail fish market, bait shop and ticket center while he was running the popular charter fishing boat, the Miss Cape Canaveral.

Our new venture featured much of the same things that people loved about the original Rusty's, fresh seafood and lots of it, with plenty of new amenities we didn't have in the Cocoa Beach location. For one, we were directly on the water. Large picture windows faced out on the scenic harbor and folks could watch the cruise ships sail by most afternoons as they peeled fresh steamed shrimp and downed glasses of cold, draft beer.

We had a bigger kitchen, as well, and expanded our menu to include items we could never get away with in the small, overworked kitchen space at the Rusty's down south. We also had more room; Rusty's at the Port was quite a bit bigger than the Cocoa Beach location and featured room for private parties and an outside deck for late night or catered affairs.

We also had a built-in audience, with local fishermen in from a day on a chartered boat or their own, looking to taste a little of that fresh seafood they'd spent all day chasing out in the Atlantic.

We also had name recognition going for us. I wouldn't exactly call us a "chain" restaurant, by any stretch, but the success of the first Rusty's in downtown Cocoa Beach meant that folks knew they could trust a second location farther north, which might have accounted for why Rusty's at the Port opened strong – and stayed strong.

Chapter 16:

When God Closes a Door, He Opens an Oyster Bar!

I can't remember the exact date, though it would prove a momentous decision for my family and I, but I must have realized sometime in the mid-90s that I wanted to sell the Surf. Over and above the implications of closing down a family business that had kept my family, and hundreds of other families, fed for nearly 50 years, I had to think of the future.

Specifically, I had to think of *my* future.

I wasn't getting any younger, and the restaurant business wasn't getting any easier, that's for sure. The world was changing, and Cocoa Beach was changing as well.

People wanted new and different, they wanted cheap and quick, and the Surf had always been of two minds: making the "regulars" happy and keeping the tourists coming back, year after year.

The trouble with change is that it drove the regulars crazy and you never knew what the tourists were going to like from one busy season to the next. When you've built a brand like the one the Surf had in the mid-90s – family place, lounge, fine dining, celebrations, events, catering, history, legacy, etc. – you couldn't just turn on a dime like a speed boat and embrace the future at the speed of light.

No, you had to turn slowly, very slowly, like a giant steam liner or cruise ship. And a lot of times, if you turned too slowly, or even in the wrong direction, you might as well be on the deck of the Titanic!

I always complained to my family and friends that if you raised the price of a menu item by a nickel, the regulars would be out front picketing five seconds after they paid the bill. And forget about raising it by a dime; they'd come for you with tar and feathers, if not torches and pitch forks!

I wasn't sure how long I could stand in the middle of the road

– between tradition and change, between the regulars and tourists – without getting squashed by oncoming traffic.

And yet, as always, it was a good problem to have! The Surf was doing well enough, the original Rusty's was still packing them in and Rusty's at the Port was more than holding its own, succeeding among several competing restaurants in "the Cove" dining area of Port Canaveral.

Even so, I knew that despite the success of both Rusty's locations, the one downtown and the one at the Port, I wasn't up to starting, let alone running, a franchise for the next ten to twenty years. Would I like Applebee's kind of money? Sure!

Did I want their kinds of headaches? Hell no!

To me, I like things neat and tidy. I figured I could sell the Rusty's at the Port, keep the one running downtown until I sold the Surf, and then be out of the restaurant business, free and clear, sometime in the mid-2000s when I would be about retirement age. Plenty of time to enjoy traveling to places I'd always wanted to go, play golf as often as I wanted and follow the annual FSU football season in Tallahassee and spend summers, maybe even a few more winters, in Beech Mountain, North Carolina.

Nice, neat and simple.

Of course, rarely does life work out that way. And in this particular case, I sure am glad it didn't…

When God Closes a Door, He Opens a… Raw Bar?!?

Sometime in the late 90s, I had finally found a buyer for Rusty's at the Port. It was good timing for me, personally, and the perfect solution, professionally speaking. Two restaurants were a lot for me to handle, and I was thinking of slowing down, not ramping up. But now I had a decision to make. I thought if I was going to make the most impact on a sale at the Port, I needed to close the Rusty's downtown.

Essentially, I didn't want to have two oyster bars competing with each other. Not only did I figure that a buyer who knew he had the only "Oyster Bar" in town would be more partial to a big dollar sale, but on my end, what if the guy who bought the new Rusty's tarnished its reputation or served less than stellar food? I didn't want "my" Oyster

Bar diminished by his or hers, so like the folks on *Seinfeld*... I decided to get out while I was on top!

This all made perfect sense to me: I could sell Rusty's at the Port, run the Surf and use the space down in the "old" Rusty's for another new venture, something beachy and fresh and fun for the regulars and tourists alike. Then, after a few more years of fun and profit, sell the whole kit and caboodle and get out while the getting's good.

Super. Fine. Well, I'm glad all that's taken care of!

There was just one little snag (naturally): while Rusty's the Port was for sale, we had a confidentiality agreement with the potential new owner so that no one would know about the sale until it was finally official.

Makes sense: you don't want your employees to know about the sale until it's all said and done in case it doesn't go through and they end up leaving you anyway. Or their morale suffers, or they think you're keeping secrets from them, or deserting them, or any number of reasons.

Well, fortunately for us – although to me it seemed like a real disaster at the time – the prospective owner had gone out and hired himself a new chef to manage the Rusty's at the Port kitchen.

Now, as I've said repeatedly, Cocoa Beach is a small town, and the restaurant business is smaller still. I can't walk into a restaurant in this town and not see someone who used to work for me, or someone who might next week!

Now, the prospective owner himself was a fairly quiet guy, but he'd shown what I considered a decided lack of judgment in hiring his new kitchen manager. Because not only was this former chef a big drinker, but even worse, he was a big talker.

Day after day, drink after drink, he would sit at Rusty's at the Port – or "his" bar, as he started referring to it – and telling everyone in ear shot he would soon be their "boss".

The minute I heard that, I called the realtor and told him, "Deal's off. There's no way would I ever sell to a guy who couldn't keep his mouth shut for the couple of weeks it took to close the deal."

I mean, not only was the confidentiality issue blown sky high, but so was my confidence in that particular buyer. He may not have said anything about the sale himself, but his new employee – and direct representative – had, and that was enough for me. No sale, no deal and, unfortunately, no prospects for other buyers at the time, either.

At the time, I was sincerely devastated. All my careful planning, all the thought and effort I'd put into putting Rusty's at the Port on sale, quietly, confidentially, and finding a buyer had just flown out the window. But as I hear so often in church, "When God closes a door, he opens a window…"

As I stare out my office window at the cruise ships at their terminals today, from my office high above the new and improved Rusty's at the Port, I can only shake my head and thank my lucky stars the sale *didn't* go through.

Otherwise, once I sold the Surf, where would I go every day?

Seriously, though, it was a great lesson in how keeping an open mind is really the only way to survive in this business or, for that matter, in *any* business.

Chapter 17:

The Beginning of the End… Or Just the Beginning?

Another thing I've learned in this business is that sometimes you just have to take a few days off, play some golf, watch some football, take some solid council from close friends and family, and then come back recharged and renewed to face your current situation with a brand new perspective.

And that's exactly what I did when the Port deal collapsed. Quietly, slowly, carefully, I reevaluated my position and decided to keep Rusty's at the Port open and growing while at the same time offering the Surf up for sale instead.

Closed door? Meet open window!

It took awhile. I mean, it wasn't like it happened overnight. There were a few buyers along the way, even a few friends who thought they might make a go of it, but eventually they realized that they would have to do one of two things to make the Surf survive without a Fischer behind the wheel, or the bar, for that matter: work the same constant hours I did to make it their "own," or try something completely different.

Eventually, most people didn't really want to do either. Not that I could blame them. Just as Bernard's shoes felt too big to fill when I took over for him in the 60s, I'd worked hard to build a brand that was as personal to me as it was professional.

It would have been hard for anyone to step in and just say, "Oh, Rusty's not here anymore." And, no matter how desirable its location might have been to prospective buyers, it would be just as challenging to change the name, wipe the slate clean and start from scratch.

The End of an Era

Downtown Cocoa Beach is as finicky as it is funky, eclectic, loyal and diverse. You've got tattoo parlors next to souvenir stands next to health food stores next to ice cream parlors next to jazz clubs next to cigar bars next to sushi bars next to bicycle shops and more.

But each of the businesses who survive, even thrive, in downtown Cocoa Beach have worked hard to carve out a niche that works for them. Even some of the big chain restaurants who came sniffing around thinking they might make a go of it balked at the sheer size, and legacy, of the building at 2 South Atlantic Avenue.

But eventually we did find a buyer, a couple of guys who felt they had the youth, energy, enthusiasm, skill, know-how, entrepreneurial spirit and the right financial backers to make a new version of the Surf work in their favor.

For me, it was a tough, but inevitable, decision. I could write a whole book about the various pros and cons I considered during the intervening years it took for the Surf to sell, let alone a single chapter. But at the end of the day, it was more a gut feeling than a series of cold, hard facts. I could stare at spreadsheets all day, crunch the numbers all night, but nothing was going to change the way I felt about the decision I'd ultimately made.

For better or worse, right or wrong, it was simply the right time to sell; for me, for the business, for my family and ultimately for my future. Hospitality is a young man's game, and my days of walking the floor two shifts a day, six days a week, were inevitably drawing to a close.

I was looking for a change. Not necessarily retirement, per se, but something new, something different, something surprising after so long spent in one place, doing one thing, day after day. And, not for nothing, something I hadn't necessarily chosen for myself all those many years ago. Bernard's prolonged illness and my family's request to run the Surf in his stead had been an offer I literally couldn't refuse. And yet, all the same, I couldn't deny the fact that running the family business hadn't been my first choice. Frankly, it hadn't been my choice at all. Now, suddenly, I was making the biggest decision of my life.

And, for better or worse, the choice was all mine…

And so we proceeded with the sale of Bernard's Surf, doing our due diligence, handing over paperwork, crunching the numbers, haggling out the details, until finally an agreement was reached, one I would be happy with regardless of how "the Surf" succeeded, or failed, in my absence.

It was a cash deal, for me, and what the buyers were actually purchasing was the land I owned, not the restaurant per se. Still, like myself before them and Bernard before me, it wasn't just land they were buying, or a building or the supplies to make a restaurant run, but a legacy. And that didn't really hit me until it came time to sign the paperwork at the closing and call the deal "done," once and for all.

I can tell you I had more than one sleepless night in the days before, and particularly after, the ink was dry on that particular contract. I couldn't help but wonder: Had I done the right thing? Was I rushing this? Could I actually give all this up?

I mean, I lived off of Minuteman Causeway and to get anywhere in town, left or right on A1A, I'd have to drive right by the Surf. Could I do that every morning, and not pull into the back parking lot, grab a cup of coffee and make my rounds, like I had every day for the last five decades or so?

And even if I could… would I *want* to?

Still, once the deal was done, there was no looking back and, actually, in my last few days at the Surf, I was kind of feeling more at ease with the idea of leaving my home away from home than I ever thought I could be. There was no turning back now anyway, and so as I made those few last rounds, on those few last shifts, I eventually decided to change my perspective. I quit regretting the things I couldn't change and focusing on the future that I could.

Gradually, I quit fearing what I might have done differently and embracing the decision I'd ultimately made. Every time I walked by a leaking dishwasher or past a complaining customer or messy table that needed to be bussed, I don't mind telling you, I was more than a little relieved.

And so the day finally came when I would own the Surf no more. The business never closed, officially; it just merely changed hands. Quietly, officially and inevitably. The actual day was November 16, 2006, at 11 o'clock in the morning. Tonya Morgan was there, pretty much steering things for the new owners the way Norma and Ana Mae and Stan had for me when I took over from Bernard way back in the 60s.

For those unfamiliar with the name, and shame on you, Tonya is the niece of one of Cocoa Beach's finest mayors, the much loved – and much missed – Joe Morgan. Tonya also hails from restaurant blood, as her father Tim Morgan used to own the equally beloved Alma's restaurant just a few blocks down from the Surf, before they faced the same decision I was facing now and sold it as well.

Tonya had been a manager for me for years, loyal, professional, firm, fair and like most people I hired, just plain fun to work with. When she learned that I'd be selling the Surf, and focusing my efforts on Rusty's at the Port in its wake, she was eager to follow me out there.

Naturally, I couldn't wait to bring her along. But part of the deal with the new owners was they needed someone strong and vital like Tonya to stay behind, for at least a full year, to ensure some continuity in the operations and make sure things ran as smoothly as possible.

Naturally, Tonya had agreed to the terms and so that's who basically took the reins come 11:01 AM when I walked out of the Surf, never to return.

At least, not as its owner, anyway.

You Don't Have to Go Home, But You Can't Stay Here...

The night before the Surf was officially "sold," I closed the restaurant as I had most weeknights for as long as I can remember. Despite everything that was going on behind the scenes, out on the dining room floor, in the front of the house, all was as it ever was.

In fact, it was an uneventful night for pretty much everybody but me. Decent dinner, no red flags, no brush fires, nothing ran out, all in all, a pretty good way to go out of the restaurant business!

There was a moment there, though, just before the dinner rush was over, that made me realize what I was doing, what it might mean, and what it might ultimately cost.

Customers sat, smiling, as they lingered over their dinners, desserts or night caps. Waitresses hustled here and there, settling bills or counting out tips. Ice clinked in glasses as bartenders poured and served, then poured and served some more.

And then I looked past them, to the walls and decor, to the barstools and the chrome, to the glasses and the framed portraits of my predecessors that hung all around the Lounge itself: Lou, Eddie, Sidney and, of course, Bernard himself. The Fischer Men, all four of them, staring back at me, big as life.

Were they okay with my decision? Would the details and the terms of the deal I'd made please them, as businessmen? As fathers? As uncles? I guess I'll never know. They were long gone by now, and it was just me and these lounge walls, staring back at me the way they always had.

How much they had changed over the years. Not just what had covered them, the god-awful wallpaper patterns of the 60s and 70s, the framed menus signed by cosmonauts, writers, actresses and other celebrities, but what these walls had seen, heard and witnessed over the decades.

For better or worse, the Surf had been the setting of many a meeting, greeting, blind date, prom, Homecoming, birthday or graduation celebration, anniversary, breakup and/or makeup over the years. How many couples had met, broken up, made up and broken up again in this very lounge?

My own son, Rusty Jr., had met his future wife, Martha, just down the stairs in the Raw Bar, finally getting up the nerve to ask her out – after a six-pack of Moosehead beer, that is! Though she'd declined that evening, he wore her down in true Fischer style and, months later, his brother Rhett was throwing Rusty a bachelor party not far from where he'd first asked Martha out on a date. Fast forward a few decades and they recently celebrated their 28th anniversary together!

How many other stories like that had been played out over the years? In quiet booths late at night, over whispered lunches or heated debates or after a few drinks at the bar? Strangers becoming friends, even couples, starting lifelong relationships that continue to this day?

How many couples owed their first date, a blind date, their best date – or even their *last* date – to a trip to the Surf? How many business deals had been made, or ended, in that booth over there? Or at the bar, over a two or three martini lunch? How many blueprints had been pored over in quiet backrooms?

How much of the Surf ended up in *Florida Today*, or *USA Today* for that matter, thanks to all those late night meetings Al Neuharth had with his trusted colleagues, planning and drinking and eating and, above all, working through ideas and inspiration all night?

How many friendships had I made here, many that I still covet to this day? How many of my customers, lifelong regulars, faces I'd seen nearly every day for decades, were no longer with us? Did their ghosts roam the halls, all these years later, watching new customers sit in their favorite seats?

I shook it off, focused on my plans for the future and headed for the front door. The time for regretting my decision was over, and the time for letting the new owners take over was at hand.

So there I stood, one foot in the past, and the other in the future. And yet, aside from the employees, of course, none were the wiser as I left that night, closing the door behind me and quietly, privately saying "goodbye" to an old friend that had been very, very good to me.

I'm not sure which bothered me more as I drove home that night: the fact that no one really noticed me leaving for one last time, or that it was so easy for me to walk away from a place that had been such a big part of my life for so very, very long.

New Owners, New Legacy, New Problems

The next day was a Thursday, and I didn't even go into the restaurant that morning. My longtime accountant and good friend Maury Gralla and I went to the closing with the new owners. After the deal was done and the paperwork was signed, Maury and I went to Murdoch's in Cocoa Village and had a Bloody Mary to celebrate.

It was a calm, bittersweet but not overly solemn affair. Maury had been there from the beginning and it only seemed fitting that he be there at the very end. When our drinks were done we simply shook hands and went our separate ways. Then I went and played golf, like I have pretty much every Thursday for as long as I can remember. And, honestly, I never looked back.

It's not that I didn't care about what happened to the Surf, it's just that I had made my decision months, even years, earlier and had had all that time to live with it. Now that the deed was done, what was the sense of looking back?

I was happy where I was at the Port. The future looked bright there and, after a few weeks off, I'd be ready to set up shop in the upstairs office over the restaurant and see what needed to be done to bring a little of that old Fischer magic to the "Rusty's North".

I wasn't leaving the restaurant business necessarily, just shifting gears. For now, the Surf was in my rearview mirror and it wasn't out of disrespect that I didn't want to sprain my neck looking backward, it was just that that chapter of my life was over. As the great Satchel Paige once said, "You can look back… just don't stare!"

Of course, I wanted to stay abreast of how the new guys were treating the employees, and maybe that was why I still went there every Friday for lunch after the Surf had been sold. And occasionally even Friday dinners. And it wasn't uncommon for me to pop in for a drink on the way to, or from, some event or function. Often I'd buy the regulars a drink at the bar, and I stayed friendly with anyone, and everyone, involved.

But even then, I knew it wasn't "my" place anymore, and I was more than all right with that. As part of their contract, the new owners had the right to use the "Bernard's Surf" name for, I believe, up to six months after the official sale. So the handoff was fairly seamless, at least from the outside. Business went on as usual, with the same operating hours, the same menu and even, for the most part, the same staff.

Most of the employees stayed, of course. None of them wanted to lose their jobs and the ones that followed me out to Rusty's at the Port did so voluntarily, and were faced with an uncertain future.

But for me, the future looked pretty bright indeed…

Chapter 18:

Rusty's, Take Two!

Unlike Bernard's Surf, my presence at Rusty's at the Port had neither been requested or necessary… until it inevitably was. General Manager Charlie Ragland had run it smoothly for the longest time, and I saw no reason to change that right away. But Charlie had other ideas on that topic, and for the longest time he had been begging me to at least have a more positive, proactive presence at the Port.

"Rusty," he'd say, insistently, persistently, as only Charlie could. "You've got to get up to the Port more often. I'm there most nights, me or one of the other managers, but nobody's there on Saturday night. You've got to show your face around there more often, and Saturday night is the night to do it!"

He said it so often, and was so convincing – not to mention insistent – that I finally, inevitably gave in. Now, the way the restaurant business usually works is, the longer you've been in it, the less nights, holidays and other special occasions you "have" to work. At least, in theory anyway. But I was doing it in reverse this time around. At the Surf, I was the top dog. Suddenly, at Rusty's, I was the new guy? Apparently so, because in this new, uncertain role of mine, everything had suddenly flip-flopped: not only was I working at night, but I was working on the busiest night of the week.

Well, I knew the Surf like the back of my hand. Every switch, every plug, every burner, every cooler, every shelf, every handle, every spigot, I'd used – even fixed – them all over the years. Rusty's at the Port? Not so much. And it turns out this was the wrong Saturday night to make my live "debut," I can tell you that much.

For one, half the staff didn't know who I was. With the sale of the Surf eating up a lot of my time and golf and the Seminoles eating up the rest, I hadn't spent as much time at "Rusty's North" as I maybe should have. Then again, with Charlie in place, I hadn't necessarily needed to. As a result, this old dog was suddenly the new kid in town!

After the first teenage hostess asked me if I wanted a table when I walked in the front door to start my "shift" that night, three more did before the night was finally through. I knew the building from when it was my brother Ronnie's fresh seafood market-slash-bait and tackle shop for the Miss Cape Canaveral. But as a restaurant? I was on new, uncertain ground – if you can imagine that!

And it's the little things you like to be able to do to help out that were all wrong, for me anyway. At the Surf, I knew which beer was in which cooler, where they kept the mustard packets or the plastic silverware for to-go orders.

It wasn't like I'd never worked at Rusty's before, but not the intense way you want to be able to help when your staff is in the weeds and you're standing there in your golf sweater and don't even know where the straws or the coasters are!

To make matters worse, the kitchen was all kind of backed up. Whatever was wrong that night, was wrong in a big way and by the time we all noticed, well, it was too late to fix things. Dinners were taking 35, 45, 50-minutes long, the place was packed, there was an hour wait, I felt like it was 1965 all over again and the whole place was just waiting for me to drop a tray full of food I was expediting all over the dining room floor.

I'm not sure if you've ever worked in a restaurant before, but chances are you've dined in one or two – or two hundred or more. And if you'll ever stop to notice, there's usually one table that no matter what the server, the manager or even the owner does, nope, they're not having it, there's nothing that's going to satisfy them.

Well, I had one of those that Saturday night. They were six girls on spring break from Virginia, and nothing we did worked out right for them. Their food was too hot, too cold, overcooked, undercooked, took too long, came out too fast, whatever it was, nothing worked out right.

And at these tables, there's always the "head" of the table, the one customer who seems to lead the rest into battle, calling out louder, complaining more often, and more aggressively, than all the others. Well this table had their "head," and man was she nasty. I've handled my share of rowdies and drunks before, rough necks and reviewers and irate customers, but this gal gave me a run for my money that night, let me tell you.

Finally, I just gave up. There's a point where if you keep trying to explain, to console, to plead and beg, you're just making things worse. I comped the table, comped the meals, comped the drinks, and still they weren't happy as they left, and let everybody know it on the way out the door, let me tell you.

It was just one table out of a hundred or so we turned that night, but it stuck with me still and you can bet it was the first thing I told Charlie about the next time I saw him.

"No more Saturday nights for me," I explained, in a tone that said I wasn't joking, and he got the point.

Active Retirement

After that night I took it easy for awhile. I was in a kind of "career limbo," making up for lost time on the golf course and spending quality time with my family and friends and just generally taking it easy.

You could say I missed the Surf, and particularly the people who worked and ate there, but it wasn't like I was a stranger, after all. Most Fridays I wound up there anyway, eating with friends and viewing life from the other side of the table as a customer.

Sure, it felt funny the first few times, watching the new owners do things you might not have done, making changes you might not have made, but eventually… I got used to it, and could enjoy just walking in and letting someone else worry about the constant headaches of running a business for a change.

Life went on, and I began to consider retiring for good. It wasn't like I didn't have plenty to fill my days. My then stepdaughter's son, Jack, my first and so far only grandchild (!) was a joy to behold and kept me busy with various tee ball and soccer and baseball games.

I'd invested some of the money from the Bernard's Surf sale in a package store in Cape Canaveral, inviting Rusty Jr.'s wife Martha to run it. On Saturdays I'd cart Jack up to the liquor store and pop in for a visit, picking up the deposit while Martha filled Jack with potato chips and free Sprite, echoing the way Stan Gardner used to fill up Rusty Jr. with chewing gum and breath mints all those lazy Saturdays when I used to drag him down to the Surf with me.

Then it would be up to Rusty's at the Port, where every waitress in sight would give Jack a hug... and a free Shirley Temple, heavy on the maraschino cherries. After picking up the deposit from the night before, Jack and I would have a cup of chowder and hit the road, heading off to the bank... and every spare bathroom on the way back home, courtesy of all those Sprites and Shirley Temples.

More and more often, be it consciously or subconsciously, I found myself heading up to Rusty's just the way I'd "popped in" to the Surf all those years on my days off. "Just to check on things," I'd tell myself – and anyone else who would listen, as if either of us believed me.

I didn't have a schedule, per se. At least, not in the beginning. "I'm just going to check things out for awhile," I'd tell myself, cruising past the old Surf as I turned onto A1A and head north, to the Port, passing that "restaurant graveyard" of new businesses taking up old places I used to eat in, so long ago. Soon, I supposed, Bernard's Surf – or The Surf, as it would eventually be called once the licensing deal expired – would be one of them.

It might be noon on a Tuesday by the time I got to Rusty's at the Port, just in time for the lunch rush and a quick shift behind the bar, pouring draft beers and handing out coasters (now that I knew where they were, of course). Or I might stop by after golf on a Thursday afternoon, just to check out the lay of the land and huddle with Charlie about matters big and small, pressing or long-term.

I'd walk the floor, shake a hand, listen to a story, wander up to the office upstairs, check some email, scribble out some notes and, gradually, that's how it began. Little by little, my retirement became more "active" than sedentary, until it eventually turned out I was actually retiring... from retirement! Just like old times, I began showing up earlier – and more regularly – to work in the morning.

It wasn't a spoken thing, so much, or even a conscious decision I made after such and such a time, it just felt... right. Business was booming, the Port was growing, there were questions to be answered, my youngest son Rhett was taking a bigger interest in the business and wanting to know more about eventually taking over, so... I slid in through the back door and started up my second life at Rusty's at the Port.

And I'm glad to say I've never looked back...

Chapter 19:

A Family Affair

For better or worse, some of my family and both of my kids have worked at the Surf – or Rusty's at the Port – at some point or another. My brother Ronnie came, and went, in those early years during the mid- to late-60s, before I had to fire the poor guy from the Surf. Although we both know working so closely together would have never worked out and he went on to bigger and much better things working for Dad on the seafood side of the business.

While Ronnie's son Ryan has never technically worked for the Surf or Rusty's, I believe he *has* been romantically linked to at least one of its servers and I suppose that counts, right?? All joking aside, I know that when and if we ever do open up that sushi bar idea he presented us with a few years back, he will be there faster than you can say "reduced sodium soy sauce"! So the jury's not out on that one yet!

Rusty Jr. got his feet wet in high school working summers at the Surf, picking shells out of endless cans of Clayton's fresh crab claws, slicing and grinding countless heads of cabbage for our homemade coleslaw and even taking a cue from his old man by making garbage cans full of fresh, homemade tartar sauce.

And what of Rhett, my youngest son? Well, that's where this predictable story takes a rather unpredictable turn:

The Youngest, The First

Rhett joined the Rusty's team completely on a whim, and totally without my knowledge. It was hurricane season, 2004, and he was living and working in Orlando when August rolled around. After graduating from Florida State with his Master's in Sports Marketing, Rhett worked here and there, doing a stint out in California with the Senior PGA Tour and returning to work for a sports marketing company here in Brevard.

Along the way he got a realtor's license, and he was busy selling condominiums by the hand full in downtown Orlando when Hurricane Charley came along and did millions of dollars of damage in the Central Florida area, blowing Rhett's career as a real estate magnate off course in the process.

Condo sales slowed to a crawl as sliding glass doors needed to be replaced and water damage repaired and with thousands of homes in need of service, the waiting list was a mile long and twice as wide.

Rhett started temping at various office jobs to keep the bills paid and one day, while stuffing envelopes and licking stamps, he'd finally had enough. He called his old pal, and former Rusty's manager, Tonya Morgan and asked if he could pick up a few shifts at night tending bar.

She happily said "Yes, come on down" and so he did, picking up stakes and moving back to Brevard. We're not exactly big on communication in the Fischer family, in case you haven't already guessed, and I think the first hint I got that Rhett had returned to the Rusty's fold was when I walked in one afternoon and saw him standing behind the bar, pouring a draft beer in his Rusty's uniform.

"Hey son," I might have said, perhaps a little surprised.

"Hey Dad," he might have replied, perhaps a little sheepishly.

And that was that. But secretly, of course, I was glad Rhett was back at Rusty's, and he seemed to be too. From a few shifts a week just to make ends meet he began picking up more and more, until finally he was working there full time.

Weeks turned to months, months turned to years – that happens in a family, and especially in a family business – and finally Rhett was just as much a part of Rusty's at the Port as I was.

One day, it wasn't planned, and I'm not sure if he'd been thinking about it for awhile or perhaps it just occurred to him, he said to me, "Dad, I could see myself running this place someday..."

And that was my first inkling that, finally, at long last, at least *one* of the Fischer kids was going to one day take over the family business. Was I surprised that it was my youngest kid? The one with a surfboard in every room and enough tattoos to fill a wall mural?

Listen, after over fifty years in the restaurant business, nothing much surprises me anymore...

All in the Family

But it's not just *my* family that made the Surf special over the years, and continues to make Rusty's at the Port just as unique as I gradually warm to the second phase of my life as a restaurant owner. It's the families that choose to make Rusty's their home, and a family business all their own.

Many of the folks who start at Rusty's gradually fold their family into the workaday mix. Tonya Morgan started at the Surf and eventually migrated up to Rusty's at the Port, bringing with her both daughters, Olivia and Sophia, and even her son Morgan, to work alongside her for a spell. Tony Greenwell, longtime bartender, convinced us to hire both his daughters, Chelsea and Monica, and son Blaine, and we're sure glad we did. Other Greenwells have made significant contributions to the Rusty's fam as well, including David and his mother Sabrina, as well as Shannon Greenwell, server, bartender and TikToker extraordinaire!

And even though Maria Meagher has long since quit catering for the Surf, and Al Neuharth, she was gracious enough to recommend her daughter Michelle and son Michael, both of whom were regular fixtures on the Rusty's deck during their time as part of the Fischer family business. (And, as luck would have it, we were happy to recently welcome Mike back into the Rusty's fam!)

And even those who no longer work at Rusty's, in the restaurant business or at all, still stop by to make some random day doubly special. It might be Bo Pete, from the Surf era, stopping by to have a basket of his favorite fish and chips and reminisce about the good old days at the Surf.

Who knows? It might even be you. Many is the time I'll be walking the floor and someone will come up to me and say, "Remember me...?" I must confess I don't always do, but that only gives them the opportunity to remind me that they still come by every year, to order a favorite dish or to watch the cruise ships go by as they sip a margarita on the deck or simply to pick up a souvenir sticker or t-shirt on their way home. Believe it or not, it's those little moments, spread out over a lifetime of many such moments, that remind me why I've been doing this for so long in the first place.

I must confess, when I started out in this business, I never quite thought it all the way through to the end. In fact, I wasn't thinking of much at the time other than making it through each shift and wondering when my father would say it was okay to go back to FSU so my "real" life could begin again.

And even when destiny called and I had to officially take over the business, I was still more concerned with learning the ropes than focusing on the future. For me, the future was the next liquor order, the next steak count, the next employee that might call off work and who might replace them.

Only after a few years, maybe even after a few decades, did I finally look up from learning those ropes to recognize what the restaurant business was all about. It wasn't about shipments and orders and payroll and processing, all of which are vitally important, no doubt.

It was about people.

The people who work alongside you to create a pleasant dining experience for the people who come to visit your restaurant for an hour or two on a random night. And even more than that, it's about what those people bring with them, and take away.

How can you help the people who work for you?

How can they help you?

Can you make it easier for them to get to work? And then get back home at the end of the day?

Can you provide a safe, happy and healthy work environment?

Can you pay them fairly in the kitchen? Or give them the opportunity to make the best money possible if they're working the floor?

Can you get to know them personally, one by one, and find out what it is that brought them to your place of business, and why they stay?

Because the more you can do for the people who work for you, the better they'll be to the people who come visit you. That doesn't just go for the restaurant business but, I believe, any business.

And if you're like me, if you've given your life to an industry, and two restaurants, and the hundreds of people who've been on your payroll and the thousands – possibly hundreds of thousands, if math was my thing – who've come through your doors, sat at your tables and eaten your meals over 50-plus years, it's more than just a business anyway.

I probably wouldn't have chosen the restaurant business if my life had gone according to plan. I probably would have stayed at FSU, gotten a degree of some kind and then coached the first sport that became available. Maybe. Possibly. The truth is, I'm not sure what I wanted to be when Lou asked me to "come help the family out" back in 1965, but it definitely wasn't "head steak counter or bottle washer," that's for sure.

But over time, as I've grown comfortable in my skin and happy in my work, I'm glad the choice was all but made for me. I could've gotten out anytime I wanted, back in the 60s, the 70s, and even when I sold the Surf in the 2000s, I thought I *was* out.

But obviously the business is in my blood, or maybe it's just the people who make up the business. Either way, I wake up every morning with no regrets. I've worked hard to run a good business, be a good boss and provide a great dining experience, and hope I've succeeded on all counts!

I guess time will be the final judge, but as long as I'm still around I'd like to think that Rusty's at the Port will continue the Surf tradition of bringing quality seafood to happy customers at reasonable prices. And if not, come see me and we'll talk about how to make your next dining experience at Rusty's twice as special.

(Or, on second thought, go see Rhett... it's his turn to handle customer complaints for the next five or six decades!)

Epilogue:

(Still) Working the "Launch Shift"

This book began with a launch and so I suppose it is only fitting that it should end with one. Well-known names like Alan Shepard, Wernher Von Braun and John Glenn peppered the beginning chapters of this story, but now new names have taken prominence in the modern space age.

Game-changers like Elon Musk and even Jeff Bezos have come to prominence in the last few years and are at the forefront of many brave men and women defining the new path of our modern era of space travel and exploration. While the VAB still stands tall as a landmark at NASA headquarters, new buildings presided over by the likes of SpaceX and Blue Origins now dot the landscape of a very modern and evolving Space Coast.

Where once I could look out over a sea of short sleeve dress shirts complete with pocket protectors milling about the Surf dining room and know it was a launch day, now when I see engineers and space techs in Rusty's at the Port, they are wearing the recognizable black and red SpaceX Falcon 9 t-shirts as a symbol of pride while working for a new, cutting-edge space company.

And so it was recently that I heard a distant rumble and instantly knew what it was. Walking out onto the deck outside my upstairs office, I could still see the fiery glow of a rocket soaring up into the sky, its bright glowing beacon sailing over Port Canaveral and soaring up and far beyond.

It reminded me of the many countless launches I watched standing in front of Bernard's Surf, one hand shielding my face as the day crew and I watched history unfold in the skies above Cocoa Beach. As this new, thoroughly modern rocket rumbled along on its high-tech trajectory, leaving behind a spiral of telltale smoke, I was instantly transported to that Melbourne High School auditorium so many years ago.

The blue Florida sky was then, as it is now, clear and bright as the rocket rumbled high above and I remembered so many launches, over so many years, so many emotions rushing to mind, all of them proud to live where I do, to do what I do, with the people and even *for* the people who launch those very rockets into space.

Who could have guessed all those years ago, from that first launch I witnessed in 1951 to some random SpaceX launch on some weekday in 2021, that I would still be watching the crowd below me giving a standing ovation to a new era of rocket launchers and history makers?

Manuscript, Interrupted

Not to flatter myself, but I know that many of you have been waiting for this book for a long time and while the rough draft was finished several years ago, my collaborator and I were forced to set it aside when the pandemic known as Covid-19 reared its ugly head and put everything my family and I had built into question.

As the country began locking down in March of 2020, Rusty's at the Port was forced to "temporarily" close its doors late one afternoon, along with dozens of other businesses in and around Brevard County, with no guarantee that any of us would ever open again.

None of us knew what we were facing then, or what might happen in the future, near or otherwise. At the time, the Rusty's team and I were faced with a looming question: When would we reopen, if ever?

True to their nature, they hunkered down, improvised, adapted and overcame and we were able to reopen a little over a month later to a very rocky future. Little by little, guest by guest, precaution by precaution, we were able to mask up, clean up and open up and welcome guests back to enjoy the full Rusty's experience, as long as they didn't mind sitting six-feet away from other guests and having their servers wear masks – and latex gloves – while they brought them their lunch or dinner.

As we all know, Port Canaveral is a working port, famous not just for its shrimp boats and trawlers but also for its glittering, gleaming cruise ships, sailing past Rusty's on an almost daily basis bearing festive guests dancing to steel drum music and waving at the crowded deck as they pass by.

All that ended in Spring of 2020 and, as of this writing, is only now just getting back to a very shaky and uncertain return to service. With the cruise ships empty and the Rusty's deck all but deserted through most of the rest of 2020 and even well into 2021, it wasn't the cruise industry that helped bring guests back to the Port and have them excited about an outdoor dining experience as America began to slowly reopen for service, but the new and exciting space program just then ramping up to speed.

One by one, launch by launch, the rockets started going up again and guests started returning, eager for something to cheer on during these desperate, uncertain times. Some symbol of hope that all was not lost and that things would eventually return back to normal – and then some!

And so it was that, on that random weekday, as I stood on the railing outside my office and gazed down at a deck full of cheering guests, I realized that as much as things had changed in the 60 plus years I had been in the restaurant business, things were still very much the same.

Just as my father Lou and I had stepped in to shape Bernard's legacy at the Surf, soon my own sons, Rusty Junior and Rhett, along with their co-owner Dana Mrdjenovich, would face the task of shaping Rusty's now and into the future. While I'm still happy to work my lunches, in this case a "launch shift," and make the big decisions that affect our business in the long run, I am more than content to watch as my three partners run the day-to-day business in their own unique and inventive ways. Unlike Bernard before me, however, I'm fortunate enough to still be here to watch my legacy unfold as we all work together to face a still uncertain future.

Back to the Beginning

And so, here we are, right at the end. And, in many ways, right back to the beginning. As I sit here typing these last few words, a rare cruise ship slides by outside my office window at Rusty's at the Port.

It might not be filled to capacity, yet, but is still heading out to the same blue seas my Dad and his three brothers, Bernard, Sidney and Eddie once braved, reeling in fishing nets and wading around in rubber boots, looking back at an unspoiled Florida coastline way back in the mid 1940s.

So much has changed since then – for them, for their children and grandchildren, for the coastline they stared back at, for the community, for the country.

And yet… so much has stayed the same.

For me, I'm surrounded by their ghosts. My office walls feature old pictures of the "Fischer men," trapped forever in sepia colors and their 40s and 50s garb, and the many awards they won over the years, and continue to win even though all four are long gone.

Just the other day, in fact, my son Rhett and my brother Ronnie went to a meeting of the Brevard County Farmers Bureau to receive a posthumous award to the Fischer family for their early efforts at aquaculture while the four brothers were still together at the Port.

Outside my door our new office manager, Ana Rivera, sits where so many sat before her: Norma Shroble, Ana Mae Petit, Jane Vester and Tere' Beaudreau, making sure the employees – and even their boss! – get paid.

Next to her sits Martha, Rusty Jr.'s wife, making sure Ana has what she needs to get the job done and that the rest of us have enough hand sanitizer, career counseling and the personal hand-holding and attentive listening for which she is so famous.

All day long my loyal and trustworthy managers filter through the office, providing updates, problem solving and plenty of comic relief. Under the strong guidance of General Manager (and, now, part owner!) Dana Mrdjenovich and floor managers Jared Hamilton, Luke Mrdjenovich, Ashley Hayes, Lori Jones and Rusty Jr. keep Rusty's at the Port running, growing and expanding at a blistering pace.

Didn't I mention that "Junior Rusty," as my grandson Jack calls him, has come back into the fold, too? Well, just like with Rhett, Junior showed up one day wearing a Rusty's uniform, having spoken to Dana and Rhett a few days earlier about joining the family business. It was another surprise – a pleasant one, at that – and to see my two sons working side by side, along with Martha, makes my heart sing.

After a few hours upstairs in the office, catching up on my emails and getting the lay of the land, I'll wander downstairs and greet the kitchen staff, filled with familiar and, due to the volatile nature of kitchen work, new faces alike.

Kitchen managers Carl Jones and Josh Turner are usually there to greet me, glancing up from doing inventory, prep work or working the front line just long enough to say "Hi" before getting back to work. And hard work it is. Fortunately, they have a staff full of competent and loyal work horses in the form of Nick Krohn, John Cordero, Joe Schaffer, Jake Tarpley, Quiana Edwards and Sally Quirk, who somehow manage to make magic happen no matter how busy or slow it is, circulating between any and all kitchen stations as proficiently as they do energetically.

I say "horses" with the utmost respect, as these friendly, fierce folks are the backbone of the kitchen, around which every restaurant is built. They work long hours and produce fast, consistent and reliable results, day in and day out, and I owe them my complete admiration for what they do behind the scenes to make Rusty's at the Port the success it is.

After a quick walk through the kitchen, I'll inevitably slip behind the bar, where I'm most comfortable, and help the day crew get through the lunch rush. This is, perhaps, my favorite part of my "new" retirement, working hand in hand with a new batch of bartenders I've literally watched grow up in the restaurant. Part of what makes Rusty's a "family" business, in more ways than one, is our insistence upon hiring from within before looking without when it's time to fill an open position.

For instance, when our hosts and hostesses and bussers turn eighteen, they typically move on as servers for a while before eventually becoming bartenders. So now a whole slew of kids we hired at sixteen and seventeen are, years later, rubbing shoulders with me on a daily basis (whether they like it or not!), pouring draft beers, shucking oysters and blending cocktails like pros.

Former server assistants like Dez and Mat, Tyler and Shannon, Sherp and Haid, constantly give me the business while I try to restock crackers and refill ice during the busy lunch rush. Naturally, I have to give it right back. I mean, hey, when your name's on the shirt, you've earned the right to want things done your way. They haven't all learned that my bark is worse than my bite yet, but they will – as long as we can put up with each other that long!

But it's not just the staff that is so familiar when it's time to clock in and get to work. The regulars are all there, of course, critiquing how I pour a beer or shuck an oyster or, lately, how I write a book chapter. (You know who you are!)

The guests come and the guests go, the Florida sun shines and the ocean laps the new waterfront deck and the dishes go out full and come back empty – and dirty.

Tables turn and servers collect their tips and bussers clean the table and servers set it back up and more customers come and order their drinks, then their meals, smile and pay, get up and leave and the pattern repeats itself, lunch, happy hour, dinner, lunch, happy hour and dinner all over again.

It's a cycle I've watched lather, rinse and repeat over and over again, year after year, for decades now. I won't say I never tire of it, but obviously I'm not too tired to come in for another day and watch it repeat itself all over again, mostly with a smile on my face.

And maybe that's the charm, after all. We're all drawn to the familiar, the comfortable, the old and the worn. While I'm looking forward to "another" retirement one day, and possibly soon, I'm not quite ready to give it all up just yet.

There is something about the clink of ice in a glass, the snap of a beer bottle opening, the hum of customers talking and laughing and chewing and chuckling that is so familiar – and comforting – to my ears I'm not quite sure what to do without it.

Besides, it's always fun to teach Rusty Jr. and Rhett a thing or two, like how to properly fill a basket of crackers atop the oyster bar or remind them when it rains to put up plenty of "Caution: Wet Floor" signs so no one slips and falls.

Farewell, Old Friends

I would be remiss in closing this book without mentioning the sad, untimely passing of two of its most lively characters – and my dearest, lifelong friends: Larry Garrison and Charlie Ragland. While I've attended more than my share of funerals over the years, these two really hit home.

Larry, whose chapter about getting a job at Cape Canaveral Hospital you read earlier on in this book, was a very dear friend who leaves behind a grieving wife and children, all of whom loved him as deeply as I did.

In the chapter he so generously, and sentimentally, wrote for this book, Larry spoke of the Surf as being his "second living room". That it was, my friend. That it was. But, for my take on the matter, Larry was like an honorary employee. Not that he ever did much work around the place, mind you, but he was there often enough to get to know all of the staff by name, and closed down the place with me many a night.

He was much, much more than that, of course. The stories I could tell of this generous, kind, funny, loyal man. The trips we took together, as friends, with our families, the rounds of golf we played and beers we drank, each and every one is a memory worth savoring and would take up more than the pages of this very book.

Among the many gifts Larry gave me over the course of his rich, full life, the best – and last – one was the gift of proximity. I was fortunate enough to be Larry's next-door neighbor during the last few months of his life, helping his wife Jan keep Larry positive, upbeat and as strong as possible with daily workouts downstairs in the condo gym – whether he wanted them or not!

You will be missed, my friend, by more people than you could have ever imagined. But, mostly, by me, by my boys and all the rest of the Fischer family.

Another huge loss I suffered before the publication of this book was the passing of my former GM, business partner and one of my very best friends, Charlie Ragland.

Like many in the Rusty's "family," Charlie had been a part of my professional and personal life for so long I just took for granted the fact that he would always be around. Unfortunately, none of us are promised tomorrow and his life was cut tragically short after what was supposed to be "routine" surgery. But I can tell you this much: Charlie and his beloved wife Nancy lived the last few years of his life to the fullest.

Their RV trips around the country were legendary and they always made sure to host their annual RV club meetings at Rusty's, making sure Charlie and I could sneak in a few moments of reminiscing along the way.

He was a frequent guest at Rusty's as well, always willing to help a newbie like Rusty Jr. out with some piece of work advice, counseling Rhett through some helpful mentorship or simply trying – and failing – to introduce a new menu item to the famously hard-to-convince kitchen staff!

While many employees worked for, then moved on, from Bernard's Surf and, later, Rusty's at the Port, it was Charlie, for the most part, not myself, who influenced them on a daily basis. He was there in the trenches, counseling them, correcting them, hiring and occasionally even firing them, on a much more intimate and personal level than I ever was.

So many former and even current employees have told me over the years how big an influence Charlie had on their lives, and I couldn't agree more: his influence was legendary, and I felt it personally for too many years to mention. Like Larry, Charlie will be missed in a massive, seismic way. Not just by me, but the entire Bernard's Surf and Rusty's family.

The Eyes Have It

Speaking of Bernard's Surf: from a corner of the Rusty's lobby a framed portrait of Bernard sits, watching over me, watching over us all, every day. Even I don't know the historical origins of the portrait, but obviously it was professionally done and it hung with pride in Bernard's Surf for years.

It shows my uncle Bernard, spiffy as ever in a black suit and tie, holding a large Surf menu and wearing his best "greeting a new customer" smile.

Few who come to Rusty's at the Port know who the man in the picture is anymore, and it certainly doesn't mesh with the rest of the seafood themed art or space-themed memorabilia that hangs around the place, from the beer posters and handmade signs (made by Rhett and his "partner in art," Lori Jones) to the autographed portraits of astronauts hanging in our "mini museum," otherwise known as the front lobby. But it hangs there just the same, and I just can't bring myself to take it down.

Some of the employees swear Bernard's eyes follow them wherever they go throughout their shift, like one of the spooky pictures at Disney's Haunted Mansion. I assume it's just the ghost of Bernard, watching over his legacy and, hopefully, smiling at its success. Because even though we're no longer in the building at 2 South Atlantic Avenue in Cocoa Beach anymore, the legacy of Bernard's Surf lives on to this day.

In me, in my sons Rhett and Rusty Jr., in my managers and employees, the kitchen staff and the customers who still come looking for what Bernard hoped to serve them over 70 years ago: fresh, Florida seafood, served in a pleasant environment at reasonable prices.

As a restaurant owner, as a Floridian, you can't ask for much more than that!

www.ingramcontent.com/pod-product-compliance
Lightning Source LLC
Chambersburg PA
CBHW032054080426
42733CB00006B/265